Sierra Leone Remembered

Esther L. Megill

First published by AuthorHouse 07/13/04

ISBN: 1-4184-5549-0 (e-book)
ISBN: 1-4184-1419-0 (Paperback)

Library of Congress Control Number: 2004092212

Printed in the United States of America
Bloomington, IN

This book is printed on acid free paper.

This book is dedicated to
the many friends, Sierra Leoneans and
fellow missionaries,
who shared with me the experiences told here.

Appreciation is expressed to Sylvia Smyth,
who read the book and made many
helpful suggestions,
and to Helen L. Hill, for her work in
proof-reading.

Contents

Preface

Sierra Leone is located on the West Coast of Africa and covers an area of almost 28,000 miles, a little smaller than South Carolina. The population is composed of many ethnic (tribal) groups, which speak a total of fourteen languages and many more dialects. English is the official language and Krio (the language of the Creoles), is widely spoken. It is a mixture of English with smatterings of French and Portuguese, and is often a literal translation of the vernacular.

Little is known about the early history, or exactly when the various tribes came to Sierra Leone. The Portuguese sighted the coast of Sierra Leone in 1446, but it was sixteen years before the coastline was mapped by Pedro de Sintra. He called the country *Serra Lyoa*, or Wild Mountain. Others have said that *Sierra Leone*, as it became known, means "Lion Mountain," but the Portuguese Governor of Elmina Castle, Ghana, disputed that fact, saying that de Sintra himself told him that he called it *Serra Lyoa* because the land looked so rough and wild, not because it was inhabited by lions.

The Portuguese settled at Port Loko, and traded kola nuts, ivory, and slaves. The ships of other European nations began to arrive. Although they were rivals, the Portuguese, French, Dutch, and English were interested in trade rather than in settling in the country. During the eighteenth century about three thousand slaves were sold every year from the area around Sierra Leone. The modern history of Sierra Leone began when slaves who had been persuaded by the British to leave their masters in America and go to England were settled in 1787 on a hill near the "watering place." For many years ships paused here on their journey up the Sierra Leone River to take on water and supplies. There was little shelter, and many died when the rains began.

The Sierra Leone Company was founded in England in 1791. The purpose of the trading company was to provide Africa with the European goods rather than to perpetuate the slave trade. They began to govern the settlement which they renamed "Freetown." After the Revolutionary War in America many slaves, freed by the British army, were taken to Nova Scotia. They were dissatisfied with the bitter cold and harsh conditions. The Sierra Leone Company sent a ship for them, and they too settled in Freetown. Thus, the Colony was formed. Later, slaves who escaped from Jamaica joined them. After the British outlawed slavery the Royal Navy would stop slave ships from other countries, and take the slaves they released to the Colony. However, the Temne rulers resented their land being taken, and a war resulted. The Colony expanded into Sherbro territory.

As traders extended into the interior, the British sent soldiers to protect them. After prolonged fighting the Protectorate was proclaimed in 1896. Thus, until independence, Sierra Leone was divided into the Colony, inhabited mostly by the Creoles, descendants of the settlers, and Protectorate, where the peoples native to the country lived. However, in 1924 the Colony and the Protectorate were made jointly responsible for government, allowing three Chiefs from the Protectorate to sit in the legislature. By 1957 there was a House of Representatives, which included members elected directly from the Colony and the Protectorate.

Sierra Leone is in the tropical forest belt, although most of the original forest no longer exists. It is 18 degrees north of the equator. There are two seasons, the dry season from November to April and the wet or rainy season in the rest of the year. Freetown has as much as 75 inches of rain a year. The mean temperature is about 80° F. It is a land of small farmers. The chief exports were (until the civil war) piassava (fibers from a particular kind of palm tree used to make brushes), palm kernels, ginger; coffee and cocoa; and diamonds. There are three religions: traditional African religion, Islam, and Christianity.[1]

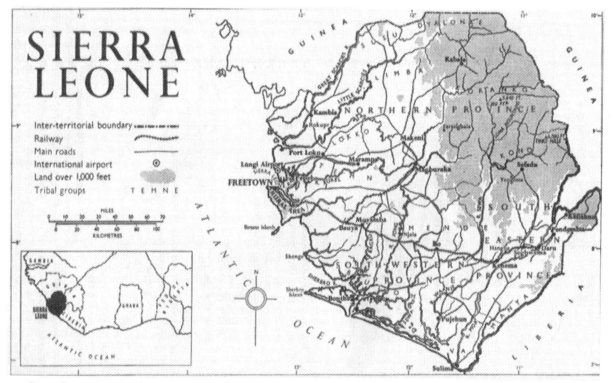

–From *Sierra Leone: the Making of a Nation*, published in 1960 in London by Her Majesty's Stationery Office.

Freetown and the rural area comprised the Colony Peninsula. The Northern, South-Western and South-Eastern Provinces comprised the Protectorate. After independence the terms "Colony" and "Protectorate" were no longer used. (Rotifunk, not shown on this map, was a few miles west of Bauya and Moyamba on the railroad.)

Prologue

Mary and Joseph Gomer–Pioneer Missionaries

Mary and Joseph Gomer stood at the rail of the ship on which they had sailed so many days ago from England, after traveling from New York to Liverpool. They eagerly watched the horizon as the sailing ship moved smoothly through the waves toward the shores of Africa. Suddenly Joseph called, "Look, Mary! Do you see them? It must be the 'Lion Mountains' of Sierra Leone!"

He took his wife's hand, and she looked up at him and smiled. Together they watched silently as the shore line came closer and the outline of the hills around Freetown became clearer and larger.

How God has guided us, thought Joseph. *Who would have thought that a black boy born on a farm in Michigan would ever find himself here?* He remembered how much he had wanted to go to school, but though there were no slaves in Michigan, black children were not welcome. Teachers looked the other way when the white children called him ugly names and tormented him in every way they could. He hadn't gone to school very often. Somehow he had learned to read and write, and a little arithmetic, English, and geography. What education he had was mostly from what he had read and learned for himself.

When he was very young, he had left home, and wandered from place to place. At sixteen, he found work in a furniture store in Chicago. There he learned to upholster furniture. It was in Chicago that he became a Christian at age twenty-five. Life truly changed for him then.

Then the War had come. Southern states rebelled against the federal government. To help save his enslaved people and try to save the Union, he joined the Union army. But of course he was still black, and even though he wore a soldier's uniform he worked as a servant, a cook for white officers.

Mary, too, was thinking how her life had changed since she had met the man standing beside her. She was returning to her home in Ohio from New Orleans, on a steamboat on the Mississippi River. Her husband had died, but her sixteen-year-old daughter was with her. She had enjoyed talking to the soldier who was returning North now that the war was over. But how surprised she was when he asked her to marry him, even before they landed in Cincinnati! She knew she had learned to love him during the days on the boat, and they were soon married, in Dayton, Ohio.

Then Joseph had found work as a foreman in a company where he supervised the making, measuring, and fitting of carpets.

They had joined the Third United Brethren in Christ Church, where they had been married. Joseph was soon known as a faithful, earnest, reliable worker in the church. He held many different offices through the years--class leader, trustee, steward, Superintendent of the Sunday School.

Then they heard that the mission board of the church was thinking of closing their mission work in Africa, the first mission work of the church outside the United States, which had been started only fifteen years before. Missionaries who went to the West African colony of Sierra Leone and the land beyond often became ill. The only missionaries had returned just the year before, and the man had died a few days later. The faithful Sierra Leonean who had worked with the missionaries had also died.

Where would they find missionaries willing to go to that land that came to be called the "White Man's Graveyard?" Who would go to tell the people about the Christ who had died for them?

It was then that the Gomers had volunteered to go, if they could be of use. But the officials hesitated. How could they send a man who had little education, and was not an ordained minister?

Finally, however, when they could find no one else, the Secretary of the Board asked the Gomers, "Will you go to Africa?"

"Yes," Joseph answered, "If you can use us at all."

Mary, too, said, "Yes, we'll go gladly."

And so here they were, after their long journey by train to New York, by ship to Liverpool, and then in another sailing ship over the stormy North Atlantic. Now they stood in the hot African sun, watching eagerly as they came closer and closer to the strange and unknown land which was to be their home. [January 11, 1871]

As the ship dropped anchor in the harbor, canoes rowed by smiling men darted out to meet them. The passengers climbed down the rope ladder into the canoes, and were carried to the shore. They were greeted by an American from another mission, and in a few days were taken by boat along the coast to Shenge, the coastal village where the United Brethren Mission had started.

There they were introduced to Chief Thomas Caulker, who received them with warm greetings. Mr. Flickinger, the Board Secretary who had been one of the first missionaries, had told the Gomers how this chief had hindered their work. He would not allow his slaves to go to the meetings or the school of the missionaries. But as the Gomers came to know him, he changed. He gave up the worship of other gods. He asked God to forgive him through Jesus Christ, and attended worship. He now encouraged his slaves to attend the meetings, and often urged his people to become Christian.

But in a few months the old man died. Mr. Gomer spent his last day with him, reading to him from the Bible. Other Christians, too, prayed and sang. The old chief was in pain, but he died speaking of salvation in Jesus Christ. The chief who followed him supported their work, though he never became a Christian.

The Gomers were very busy. They organized Sunday Schools, Bible Classes, prayer meetings, and day schools. They soon saw the need for an ordained minister to baptize, give communion, and perform Christian marriages. So the Board sent another black missionary couple [The Rev. J. A. Evans and wife], and later other missionaries. In 1876 when the Gomers returned for a short time to America he was ordained. During the few months in his own land he preached in many churches. Everywhere he went, he told the Christians of America what God was doing in Africa and how they could help through their prayers and gifts.

Joseph Gomer knew that he must not only preach the Gospel, but must also help people to live a better life. Also, they needed food for students in their schools. So, after they returned to Africa, with the help of two new women missionaries [Miss Beeken, supported by the Women's Missionary Association, and Miss Bowman], they started an Industrial School. The boys and girls cleared land to plant crops for food and to sell. There were two oxen to help in plowing and carrying loads, and sheep and pigs. There were tools for a blacksmith and carpenters; a tailor shop; and boats and nets for fishing. For girls there were sewing classes, and Bible classes for everyone.

There was much work and many problems. Leopards killed several goats and a pig. A calf was attacked one night. Hearing the noise, Joseph went out with a lantern, and shot at the leopard. He frightened it off, but the calf was so badly bitten they had to kill it.

The cow got sick and had to be killed, and the sow and two pigs died. But the school continued. One of the students [Daniel F. Wilberforce] went to college in America, and returned as a minister to serve his people. Others were faithful teachers in mission schools. Many boys learned to do useful jobs with tools, and girls became good homemakers.

Mr. Gomer was loved and respected by the people for other reasons, too. When he had been in Africa only a year he saw how the two Paramount (top) Chiefs of the Sherbro people were bitter enemies. Though they were cousins, they kept their country in constant unrest and trouble. The people took sides, and there were wars and other difficulties. Mr. Gomer, with the help of a native of the colony of Sierra Leone, was able to get the two men together and agree to be friends. They made peace in the presence of several hundred people. They all rejoiced, and the women clapped their hands for joy. Over and over the people thanked the two men, and especially Mr. Gomer, for bringing such a change. This gave Mr. Gomer great influence over the people.

For twenty-two years Joseph Gomer worked along with his wife, preaching, teaching, visiting villages, establishing schools and churches. He was kind and patient, and many people looked up to him and loved him.

It was on September 5, 1892, that Joseph Gomer arrived in Freetown, where he had gone to accompany two missionaries and help them get off to America, because of the man's illness [Miller]. He was there, too, to meet his wife, who was recovering from an illness. That evening the two men talked together, and then all had family worship together. But not long after they had gone to bed, Mr. Gomer died of a stroke.

Mary asked that his body be taken back to Shenge, as Joseph had wanted. There, as his many friends mourned, he was buried near the church he had helped to build. Even today one can see the stone church, with Joseph Gomer's grave, among others, behind it.

Mary stayed on for two more years, and though she was not well and could not do much work, the people loved her being with them. But in 1894 she said goodby to Africa, and two years later died in America.

Both had given their lives freely so that the people of Africa could know God's love through Jesus Christ.

The first view of Freetown from a ship

Gomer Memorial Church, Shenge

BIBLIOGRAPHY

This story was based upon the following materials:
Encyclopedia of World Methodism. 1974. p. 1016.

Flinkinger, D.K. and William McKee. *Ethiopia--Coming To God.* Missions of the United
Brethren in Christ. History of the Origin, Development, and Condition of Missions among
the Sherbro and Mendi Tribes, Western Africa. Dayton, Ohio: United Brethren Publishing
House, 1885.
(Includes letters by Joseph Gomer.)

Mills, J.S. *Mission Work In Sierra Leone, West Africa.* (Memorial Edition). Dayton, Ohio:
United Brethren Publishing House, 1898. (J.S. Mills was Bishop of the United Brethren in
Christ.)

The Missionary Visitor, "Rev. J. Gomer," December 8, 1892, p. 44.

Religious Telescope, "Personal," December 7, 1870.

Religious Telescope, "Rev. Joseph Gomer's Last Article for the Telescope," September 28, 1892,
p. 4.

Religious Telescope, "Rev. Joseph Gomer," October 26, 1892.
(Story of his death.)

Religious Telescope, "Rev. J. Gomer is Dead," November 2, 1892, p. 683.

Chapter I. The Adventure Begins

It was July of 1950. I had recently been commissioned as a missionary of the Evangelical United Brethren Church to go to Africa after I finished my training as a Medical Technologist, and had opportunity for more training in England. I had looked forward to this day since I quietly responded to God's call at a campfire service at a youth camp, eight years earlier.

One night as I lay on my room in the nurses' dormitory at Miami Valley Hospital in Dayton, Ohio, I began for the first time to question what I was doing–to say to myself–How can I go to a strange, faraway place–an unknown country? How can I leave family and friends?

Then, in the quietness of the night it seemed almost as if I heard a voice saying, "Lo, I am with you, to the ends of the earth." With this assurance I fell asleep.

On September 11, I left for England, my first stop on the way to Sierra Leone, West Africa. I left alone on the S.S. Media, a British ship, from New York (I, who had never seen a mountain, a forest or an ocean!), and arrived ten days later in England.

On January 4, 1951, Gertrude Bloede, who had finished her midwifery training in England, and I boarded the mailboat Accra. We arrived in Sierra Leone on January 13, eighty years after the Gomers had arrived as pioneers in this land–and our adventure began . . .

Boarding the *S.S. Media*

Gertrude and I were awake long before daylight on that day. We had been scheduled to arrive at 6:00, but were late; so when we awoke the ship was still moving. We dropped anchor before daybreak, and went on deck to catch the first glimpse of the country that was to be our home. At 8:30 we went to the immigration officers and were told that Rev. Walter Schutz was looking for us. From then on he took over and saw to our getting our baggage through customs, etc. At that time there was no dock in Freetown, so we went on a launch from the boat to the pier (after climbing down a ladder into the launch). By afternoon we had our first taste of the hot African sun, and were glad to follow "Pa" Schutz's advice and buy some helmets.[2]

I had been looking forward for months to the time when I would see my close friend Ethel Brooks, who was already working in Sierra Leone. She was not able to be in Freetown to meet me at the boat, but she arrived from Moyamba on the train at about midnight that Saturday night. So we had two wonderful days to catch up on the events of two years.

Esther Megill, Gertrude Bloede, Walter Schutz
January 13, 1951

Esther Megill, Ethel Brooks

On Tuesday morning Rev. Schutz and Ethel went with us on the train (a narrow gauge railroad). (Ethel continued on to Moyamba from Rotifunk). It is only fifty-five miles from Freetown to Rotifunk, but the train trip took four hours, and often more. We watched the lush tropical scenery go past (not very fast), and eagerly looked out the windows when we stopped at a town. There were always crowds of people, many of them there to sell oranges, bananas, or other items to the travelers. Rev. Schutz and Ethel were good tour guides, too.

Freetown to Rotifunk

Masanki Palm Oil Plantation

Curious Children

At 12:30 we arrived at Rotifunk, where Dr. Mabel Silver met us at the station. And so we were "home" at last. Ruth Harding, a nurse midwife, was also there to greet us–so we were four in our family.

Dr. Silver meets us at the train

Carrying our trunks to the house

The Rotifunk Family: Gertrude Bloede, Ruth Harding, Mabel I. Silver, Esther Megill
January 1951

The Hospital Compound

Our House

Martyrs Memorial Church

Outpatient Clinic

Maternity Ward

Male and Female Wards

Entrance to Surgical Building

Scenes in Rotifunk

The E.U.B. Primary School next door

Rotifunk Main Street

Lebanese/Syrian Shops

The Market

Going to Market

Scenes at the Riverside

Women Fishing

Swimming and
"Brooking" Clothes

The Road to Chief Town
Martha Johnson & Esther Megill

Chief Town

Chapter II. At Home in Rotifunk

"Yes, they have medicine there [in some of the government clinics],
but they don't care about people;
and when they don't care about people, the medicine doesn't have power."

My first task was to set up a laboratory, for I was the first medical technologist at the hospital. The hospital, made from cement blocks, was a "bush" hospital, and the wards for patients had only recently been completed. In addition to a ward for men and one for women, was a clinic, with the lab attached and a waiting room with benches for the crowds which gathered every day to see the doctor.

A. Max & Honoria Bailor

A small room off the clinic provided privacy for the doctor's examination when necessary. Another room off the waiting room was used to dress the many ulcers caused by such diseases as yaws, and wounds which did not easily heal when one had leprosy, or for other reasons. There were a dispensary and storeroom, a building for a surgery, and a "barrie"* where baby and leprosy clinics were held. The other building–the first built–was a maternity center, with a delivery room and beds for patients and babies. In addition there were houses for the African staff, and one large house for the missionary staff (at that time all the doctors and trained nurses were missionaries). For many years we had no electricity, so on rainy dark days I had difficulty seeing small objects, such as amoebic cysts, through the microscope. We had pressure lamps in our home and kerosene lamps in the hospital, with a pressure lamp when needed.

Our mission compound was right in the middle of the village, so we had the full benefit of all the noise and confusion. Our house (for the doctor, nurses, and med. tech–all women at the time) was on top of a hill, at the bottom of which was the railroad station. About two hundred yards from the house was the church, and on the other side of the church the new buildings, described above. Just over the low hedge that marked the end of our compound was the mission school. The buildings were not closed in (it is not necessary in that climate), and were overcrowded.

* See the dictionary in the back for a definition of terms marked with an asterisk.

All the teachers were native Sierra Leoneans. The Headmaster was Mr. A. M. Bailor, and his wife, Honoria, who became my African "sister," was one of the teachers. We as missionaries had nothing to do with the school, and we were just   members of the church, although we often acted in an advisory capacity, and I was soon asked to help with Christian education for the children.

Rotifunk was a cosmopolitan village. Temne was the dominant language, but there were also sections in which Sherbro, Mende, and Loko and Limba were spoken. Someone once said that medically all roads lead to Rotifunk. (Although at that time there were no roads–only a tidal river, the train, and paths through the bush). Dr. Silver was so famous that people were constantly coming from places even where there were doctors and hospitals. So one saw people from Temne, Mende, Sherbro, Kono, Loko, Mandingo, Limba, and other tribes, and occasionally even from other countries.

Consequently, the language situation was a little complicated! Because Sierra Leone was a British colony, all those who went to school learned English. Many understood Krio, a mixture of English with bits of French and Portuguese, often a literal translation of the traditional languages. It is really a language of its own, however, and one has to learn to understand it. We had to depend on our African staff to interpret for us–sometimes the doctor would have to go through two or three people in order to get someone who understood the language of the patient.

Rotifunk Hospital (formerly a clinic) was officially named the "Hatfield-Archer Hospital," after two women doctors, Dr. Marietta Hatfield and Dr. Mary Archer, who was also ordained. Both were sent by the Women's Missionary Association of the United Brethren Church, Dr. Hatfield in 1891 and Dr. Archer in 1895. Both these women were martyrs, along with Rev. I. N. Cain and his wife, Mary, Ella Schenck, and Arthur Ward, during the "Hut Tax War" of 1898 (as were also Rev. L. A. McGrew and his wife, at Taiama). The church at Rotifunk was named the "Martyrs Memorial Church," and there were stone plaques on the wall commemorating the missionaries who had died.

There were also stones at places in the compound where they had been killed. The uprising had begun as a protest against taxes which had been levied on each house by the British colonial authorities, and many other grievances against the new government. All aliens were attacked in a wave of fury. This included not only Europeans and Americans, but the Creole traders (descendants of freed slaves who had settled in Freetown, and the Colony) who had for many decades lorded it over the people in the interior. All government servants, and those who had adopted European ways–every man in trousers, it was said, every woman in a dress, were murdered. Thus, many Christian Africans were killed along with the foreigners.[3]

On a much lighter note: The pastor of the church frequently referred to the martyrs and the "Raid of 1898" in his sermons. At one time some of the children from the Children's Church were working on a project in my home, and one of them mentioned that Harry would have a birthday soon, and be eight years old. I said, "Yes, I remember when Harry was born."

With eyes wide open, one of the children said, "Eh, Miss Megill–you must be old! Do you remember the Raid of 1898?"

Plaque on Out-Patient Clinic

At the Taiama Bridge:

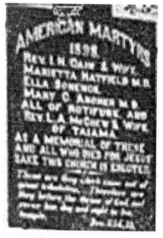

Plaque in Church

ON THIS ROCK THE AMERICAN MISSIONARIES
REV. L.A.M. McGRAW & HIS WIFE CLARA McGRAW
WERE MASSACRED
MAY 3, 1898

Our day began with services which the doctor conducted in Temne for the yard and house workers (although I am sure her day began long before that.) As we sat at breakfast, we saw patients coming up the hill in a steady stream; school boys and girls went by, carrying their books on top of their heads, and often a bottle of ink on top the books; teachers and workmen around

the hospital went by. One thing that every newcomer noticed was the variety of dress. It ranged from nothing for some children to European clothes. Women wore *lappas** and *bubas** or Creole "print"* dresses, and always carried their babies on their backs. Often they would have a big load on their heads, too. Some of the men wore flowing robes and a fez, or trousers, but many wore short pants–ranging in color from khaki to bright pink. The children who went to school usually wore European style clothes, but in out-of-school hours, or those who did not go to school, usually wore a long khaki

Dr. Silver and Ernest Kroma at work

shirt, and nothing else. This was easily pulled off and carried on top of the head if it should prove a hindrance! Little girls usually wore hip beads and earrings. Often one saw charms tied around necks, wrists, or ankles. If the babies were dressed, they were sure to have a hat, if nothing else. If they had any more clothing, there would be a dress.

I was amazed to see the work that the doctor did. From early morning people started coming to the hospital. By eight o'clock there was a crowd waiting. Before the doctor began work the hospital "chaplain" (usually one of the African staff) lead a service and talked to the people. Then the "dresser" gave "shooks" (injections) previously ordered by the doctor, took care of many other

things, and then began to call the people in four or five at a time, to the office. Of necessity the doctor gave very little time to each patient, but twenty years of experience had enabled her often to tell at a glance what was wrong with the patient. There were as many as two hundred to four hundred patients at the clinic every day.

My part of the work was in the laboratory, of course. I did examinations for intestinal parasites, urine analyses, some blood counts, smears for gonorrhea and T.B. Later, as we were able to expand the lab and I began to train a young man to help me, we were able to expand our work. Every time I looked in the microscope I

was thankful for the four months I had in England studying parasitology. Parasitology was quite rewarding–instead of being rare to find anything, as is usual in the States, it was rare not to find anything there. Almost everyone had hookworm or roundworm, or both. In addition, some had tapeworm and other intestinal parasites. We had occasional patients from other parts of Sierra Leone with bilharzia (schistosomiasis), filariasis (elephantiasis) and sleeping sickness. There was lots of tuberculosis. I always had a sinking feeling when I found the organism, for it was almost certainly a sentence of death in those first years. (Later, some new medications were discovered, which did help a number of people.) When our leprosy clinic was opened, I also did skin snips for leprosy, and later still, for onchocerciasis, which causes so much blindness.

11

Then there were the accidents–in the first months of our arrival in Rotifunk a man was brought in who had been attacked by a leopard. His companion, also a hunter, was killed. When this man heard his cries, he went to the rescue, but was mauled in several places and had a broken arm and a thumb that was almost cut off by a knife of one of his rescuers. We had no surgeon at that time, but Dr. Silver managed to take care of him and he recovered.

A more pitiful case was a man who fell from a tree and broke his back. This meant that he was completely paralyzed from his waist down. There was nothing that could be done for such cases at that time. To make matters worse, his friends had used "country" medicine on him before he was brought to our hospital four days after the accident. Their treatment was to dig a deep pit and build a fire in it. Then the fire was scraped out and the victim put in it and buried in the pit up to his neck. Because the man had no feeling from his waist down, he was terribly burned. The doctor kept him in the hospital for almost two weeks, but saw the signs of death setting in. Evidently his family did, too, for they asked to take him away. They always wanted to die at home; so the doctor let him go. We heard that he died the next day, and at the native "inquest" they found his trouble had been caused by witches! I asked Ernest Kroma, our dresser, why they should think that when they knew he had broken his back. Ernest answered, "But, you see, they think it is the witch that caused him to fall."

A month's report (February 1951) showed the work the one doctor did. She saw a total of 5,346 patients in 28 days, plus 37 inpatients. Gertrude Bloede conducted the weekly baby clinics, at which there were 685 babies (four clinics). Treatments were given for yaws, malaria, rheumatism, worms, skin ulcers, respiratory diseases, skin diseases, gonorrhea, dysentery and diarrhea, leprosy, elephantiasis, syphilis, tuberculosis and wounds–in the order of the numbers treated. (Actually, there was no treatment for elephantiasis or tuberculosis, but that was the reason the patients came to the doctor.) There were also 237 cases labeled "miscellaneous." (In addition, Gertrude no doubt delivered a number of babies, and held prenatal clinics [antenatal, in British terminology], but I have no record of those, nor of the number of lab tests I did. I do have a note that in April of 1952 I did 1,065 laboratory examinations on 773 patients.)

When the doctor once questioned a man as to why he brought his child to us and passed up another hospital, he said, "Yes, they have medicine there, but they don't care about people; and when they don't care about people, the medicine doesn't have power."

When I saw the crowds of people day after day, many of them with very terrible ulcers and diseases, I was reminded of the verse which says, "So His fame spread throughout all Syria, and they brought him all the sick, those afflicted with various diseases and pains, demoniacs, epileptics, and paralytics, and He healed them."

On February 1 of that year the new hospital buildings were dedicated. The Rev. T. B. Williams, pastor of the Rotifunk church, wrote this account of the event:[4]

The town of Rotifunk, Sierra Leone, West Africa, was the scene of an unusual concourse of people on February 1. At 2 p.m. the new hospital was to be dedicated, and many people came to witness the event.

"The pupils of Rotifunk Evangelical United Brethren Day School, numbering 380, marched in a procession to the front of the new building," writes the Rev. T. B. Williams, pastor of the Rotifunk church. The spacious waiting room which served as an auditorium for the occasion was filled to capacity by people representing the literate and illiterate, and also every shade of belief practiced in the country."

"The school children and many other spectators had to remain outside. Music was furnished by the school organ and piano accordion, which enriched the singing and made it very melodious and inspiring," reports Pastor Williams. The address was delivered by Dr. F. Maclagan, director of medical services of the Sierra Leone Government. Dr. Walter Schutz, executive secretary of the Mission, and Dr. Mabel Silver, physician in charge of the hospital, took part in the dedicatory services.

"The address," Mr. Williams says, "was replete with vital timely and practical thought. Doctors do more than talk. The Rotifunk Dispensary, with small beginning, has faithfully served the public in the ministry of healing for many years. Doctor by her skill and painstaking labours raised the status of the dispensary to that of a hospital, in recognition and appreciation of which the government donated a handsome sum of money which made possible the present modern commodious and imposing structure."

In her remarks Doctor Silver paid tribute to Miss Nora Vesper, R.N. who rendered long and faithful service to the dispensary. She organized and promoted the baby clinic which has proved such a blessing to hundreds of mothers and babies over the course of years. "It was her untiring devotion to the work," Doctor Silver said, "which made the clinic so popular and gave it such a good reputation throughout the country."

Although it took some time for beds and other equipment, ordered months ago, to arrive, and shelves and cupboards had to be built in the dispensary and the laboratory, eventually, some months later, we were all able to move into the new buildings. The Governor of Sierra Leone (British) came a few weeks later to see the new buildings, and the whole town was out to meet him. While we were going around the buildings we heard the drumming and singing of the dancers and found that a dance was in progress for the governor's benefit, right next to the hospital. That night Dr. Silver, Gertrude and I were invited to eat dinner with the Governor, his wife, the District Commissioner, and the aides-de-camp to the Governor. [Ruth Harding was gone at the time.] So we dressed up in our formals and went to dinner in the Governor's private railroad coaches.

I soon found that I had at least one trait that was admired by the people of the community. I was the first white person they had ever seen with a space between her front teeth–a most desirable trait. One of my African friends told me that people always admired it when they saw me, and I was referred to all over the village as "the young missionary with the open teeth and blue eyes."[5] Later I also learned that the three of us women–all wearing white uniforms–were designated as "the big doctor" (meaning most important), "the doctor for babies," and "the doctor that looks"–the latter because I spent so much time peering through a microscope!

Once when I was having to take some blood from a child, who of course cried, the mother said (in Krio), "Don't cry! She is only 'looking ground.'" In this way she was comparing me to the native medicine man who would scatter stones on the ground, and tell the patient what was wrong with him (and what he should bring for a cure). I thought this was quite appropriate–after all, my purpose was to help the doctor make a diagnosis!

In August of 1952 I described again a typical day at the hospital. I usually started my day at 6:00 a.m., in time to get ready for breakfast and perhaps do a little correspondence before breakfast at 7:15. At about 7:00 Dr. Silver had devotions in Temne for the twelve or thirteen

"Looking ground"

13

yard men and the three men who worked in the house for us. Immediately after that, and the orders were written on the inpatients' charts that a nurse brought over, we had our family devotions and breakfast. While we ate, we could see a procession of people going past on their way to the hospital. People began to gather as early as 6:00, so that by the time the doctor arrived at 8:30

Samuel Bendu,
Dispenser,with patient 1957

the waiting room was often full. After I had finished breakfast, I got out the food for the day, and gave instructions to the cook, etc., since I was the housekeeper for the family. Then I went over to the hospital and checked out supplies for the builders at the new house. By that time it was about 8:30, and I got ready to start my work in the lab. From that time until 12:00 or 1:00 I usually was working continuously at top speed to try to get the lab work done for the doctor before the patients got too restless because they wanted to go on the train. Then I would usually not have much to do until we quit at 2:00. Conditions were certainly quite different than in a laboratory at home. Sometimes I longed for a little uninterrupted peace and quiet when I was trying to do some work that required concentration–but such a thing seldom happened. There were interruptions of people coming into the lab with their papers and specimens to whom I had to try to talk in Krio or Mende (the only two languages I could manage at all), or by sign language to get them to do what I wanted. (As a last resort I could always call an interpreter.) Then there was always an interested audience at the windows which opened directly off my work table. Sometimes people stood right in front of me so that the light was cut off from the microscope. Or I might have a tube in my mouth and be taking a blood count from a screaming child when someone came up behind me and greeted me, expecting an answer, or announcing, "I done come!" Really, though, if one could keep a sense of humor, there were lots of things to laugh about–though it certainly could be trying, too, when one was loaded with work, everyone was pushing her, and she was dead tired! But all of us had to work under these conditions. No one can possibly imagine what it is like for a doctor to have to see from 150 to as many as 400 patients a day, speaking many different languages. And one is so limited by time and lack of money.

Rotifunk Hospital Staff January 1951

Back, L. to R.: Ernest Kroma, Dresser; Gertrude Bloede, R.N.,S.C.M.; W.C. Barley, Dispenser; Esther Megill, M.T. (A.S.C.P.); Alfred Kroma, Lab Assistant; Mabel Silver, M.D., Mary Kamara, Nurse
Front: Ruth Harding, R.N.; Edith Vandy, Nurse; Sarah Will, Nurse(Julia Bailor, Nurse, on night duty)

"They brought all the sick"

Elephantiasis

Alfred Kroma and boy with leprosy

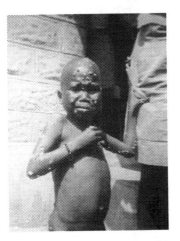

Yaws

Amoebic liver abcess

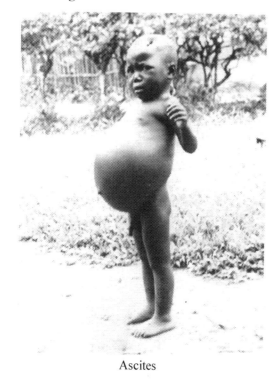

Ascites

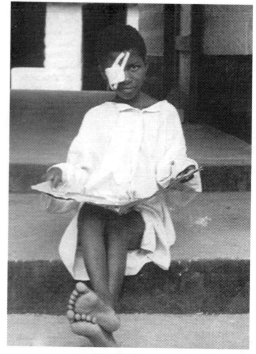

Eye Patient

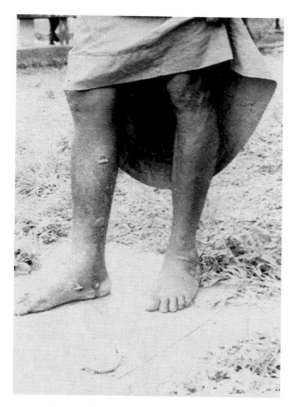

Guinea Worm (from French Guinea)

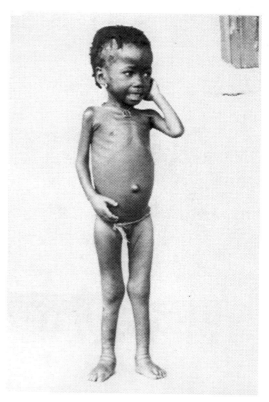

Kwashiokor

Chapter III. And Not Only Medicine--

"The gifts he gave were that some would be . . . teachers . . . to equip the saints for the work of ministry, for building up the body of Christ" –Ephesians 4:11-12

Work with Women

Though our primary task at Rotifunk was of course our work in the hospital, there were many other activities in which I was involved. I soon was asked to teach a Sunday School class of about twenty girls, ranging in age from about 9-16, although I was supposed to have only the older girls. We met under the mission house where the three of us lived, for the house was built on concrete pillars. I also helped to get a Women's Society of World Service group organized among the women. The "organization" was very slight, but we began to get the women together for meetings. At our first meeting I talked to them about the need for knowing about people all around the world, as well as the needs in our own village, and then told them the story of one of our mission schools in China. My talk was translated into Krio for them, as few of the older women understood English. It was a thrill to see how interested the women were, and how sincere they were in their prayers for people in need in other lands and how eager to learn more. They wanted to meet two times a month, and the pastor gave permission for the women to have charge of the Sunday evening service once a month. We had materials produced by a local committee, headed by a missionary Women's Worker, which we used for our meetings. Because few knew English, only a small per cent of the women could take an active part, but there were others ways they could serve. The church service, to which we especially invited the women who came to the baby clinic, was translated into three languages–Mende, Sherbro, and Temne. We observed the World Day of Prayer also. As I listened to the prayers in Krio, Temne and English, and sang (as best I could) Temne and Mende hymns, I remembered that at just that time the service would be coming to a close in Dayton, where I had recently lived. It truly gave me a feeling of the universality of our Christian religion.

Cooking rice for the Institute

In May of 1951 we had our first Women's Institute. Cora Horst, then the Director of Women's work for the Conference, came to lead it. The women from a nearby village joined our group. Honoria Bailor, already a good friend, and I worked together on the women's work, and we were very busy that day. The women had to be fed just after they arrived. Cora Horst and I were invited over to eat with them. We ate our rice and stew our way, but enjoyed watching those who ate the traditional way with their hands. That afternoon we had a meeting. Gertrude Bloede, Cora Horst, and I did the speaking, and Honoria Bailor translated into Krio. We had a devotional talk on building a Christian home, short talks on the meaning of the W.S.W.S. and Women's Work in Sierra Leone, and a talk by Gertrude on baby care. These were interspersed by choruses and hymns. How those women could sing! There was rice "chop" again that evening, and then our group (really mostly school children) gave a play which Honoria had written. They had worked very hard on it, and it was a real success. After the meeting the women came over to the mission house and had cocoa.

At 11:00 we took them to the train, everyone singing, and often dancing, until the train arrived. All in all, we felt that the Institute had been a great success, and we all had a feeling of Christian fellowship. In later years we had other Institutes.

Leadership Training

I also was asked to help that month in a leadership training program at a district rally held by the Conference. I went to Moyamba by train, and then drove by lorry (truck) with Paul Temple, the Secretary of Education for the Conference and his two children; Jim McQuiston and one of his children; and three "helpers," men to do the work to take care of meals, etc. while we were in meetings. We went to Shenge, a beautiful village on the seacoast, Honoria's home, and the place where mission work was first started by the United Brethren Church. (The Gomer Memorial Church is there, where Joseph Gomer was buried, and also Honoria's grandmother, one of the first two converts to Christianity.)

We camped in the old mission house, which was in poor condition. It is near the sea, though, and that meant a beautiful view and swimming. The rally was attended by fifty mission teachers, village workers, agents, and pastors. Rev. Temple gave lectures on school administration and methods and the meaning of worship. Rev. McQuiston had charge of the classes for the pastors on the training of seekers, evangelism, and church administration. I had charge of sessions on Christian education in the Sunday School. I had studied Christian education in college, and had held Bible Schools during two different summers for the College, so I thoroughly enjoyed getting back into that kind of work again. Dr. S. M. Renner, the Conference Superintendent, and Dr. Richard Caulker, principal of Albert Academy, the large boys' school in Freetown, planned the conference and had charge of some sessions. (They were both Sierra Leoneans.) Dr. Caulker conducted interesting discussions on community development. I was glad for the chance to learn something about the problems of the educational and evangelistic fields, as well as our own medical work. On Sunday afternoon we divided into groups and went trekking to outlying villages to hold services. Jim McQuiston and I started late, but caught up with our group at the village. We walked three miles through bush and across sandy beach. We held services in several places. I was introduced to the Chief, who shook hands with me. Then the one who introduced me said something about my working with Dr. Silver, and he shook hands again, very enthusiastically. Then we walked the three miles back to Shenge.

Paul Temple, Richard Caulker,
S. M. Renner, Jim McQuiston

Charta–One of the villages to
which we went

We went swimming two or three times a day every day. There is nothing more wonderful than swimming in the ocean at 6:00 in the morning, with the sun rising over the palm trees, unless it is swimming at night under the brilliant stars. The salt water was so phosphorescent that there were sparks every time we splashed the water. We would hold our hands up out of the water and it would look like fire flowing down our arms.

I found that my fame had spread to Shenge. Before I had left, Honoria Bailor wrote a note saying that she had written her mother and cousins there about me, but it seemed that they had already heard of me–the young missionary with the open teeth!

Work with Children at Rotifunk–The Nursery Church School

I also was later asked to help with a Children's Church at Rotifunk. Honoria and I planned together, and she interpreted into Krio when I taught. Later, teachers from the primary school were the teachers, and I supplied the materials to use and had training sessions with them. As the years went by, and I studied Christian education during furloughs, I began to write materials for use with Nursery and Kindergarten aged children, and we divided these children into separate classes, with all school children in the Children's Church.

In an article in the December 1955 *World Evangel* I wrote the following about our Nursery Church School:

It was a new experience for the 3 and 4 year olds of the Rotifunk church when they attended the first session of the new nursery church school one Sunday last March.

The two teachers who had helped me make plans for some weeks before were with me to greet the children as they came. There were Marion and Julia, half-sisters from a polygamous home; John, the pastor's child, barely 3 years, and definitely in the "negative" age; Harry, the son of our dresser in the hospital, whom I had known only on occasional trips to the hospital, when he always had a glum face and would make no responses to any approaches of friendship; Augustus, who still wants his big sister with him; Obai, who sits smiling and understands nothing but Temne; Boi and Kenya, the daughters of the chief, who speak Sherbro; and others.

I was not surprised that the children were shy that first Sunday. The situation was entirely strange to them. They had never seen a swing, or probably some, not even a doll; those who did

19

know me knew me best at the hospital which they often associated with unpleasant experiences. That first Sunday hardly a sound was heard from the children; they just sat or stood and looked. A few of the boys became interested in the sand; for the girls, the big attraction was the doll, which soon was being carried on Marion's back. When time came for church to be out, Marion cried because she had to leave the doll; so I felt that some impression had been made! For several Sundays the children were quiet and shy; some, who have not come regularly, are still that way.

But what a difference we see in others! As soon as Morlai or Phillip come, they head for the lorry (truck) and are transformed into busy lorry drivers hauling produce (and important steps have been made in learning to share this coveted toy). Harry, whose face had always been so expressionless, became a completly transformed child for me. With a mischievous twinkle in his eyes, he became an active run-about, and an exhibitionist who is constantly making a bid for attention. Marion is an enchanting child, who seems to be the center as far as her older sister and younger brother are concerned. She it is who picks up some chance phrase or happening and begins a song and dance in the typical African rhythm. Boi is still shy, but now plays some with the others; she cries almost every time she has to leave nursery class. In fact, I've said it's not often that one finds children crying to come to church, or when they have to leave!

And that, of course, is one of our main purposes in starting a nursery church school; to have a place in the church for our younger children, which they will feel is their own and to which they will enjoy coming. Other important purposes are to provide a place where they can feel loved and secure; where they can have experiences of awe and wonder at the familiar and beautiful things about them; in short, we want to give in our nursery church school an opportunity for growth mentally, physically, and spiritually so that our children will develop into the kind of people that God wants them to be. An important part of our plans for the nursery are meetings with the mothers and guardians of the children to help them understand and guide their children into more abundant life.

As the children became more familiar with the nursery class, simple stories of a little girl and boy (Fattu and Sɔba), who have experiences in home and church similar to theirs, were introduced. With the stories are used enlarged photographs of actual children who have been chosen to represent Fattu and Sɔba in making a series of pictures. Jesus was introduced to the children as a friend of little children, and that picture is often talked about. Simple songs and rhythmic play are now enjoyed by the children, as well as other activities, such as using clay and crayons.

We do not always see things happen just as we would like, and sometimes people who do not have understanding eyes cannot see, perhaps, that much is being accomplished from Sunday to Sunday in the nursery class. But for some of us, it has great promise; first, because it is a step in developing a religious education program and materials especially for Sierra Leone. And secondly, she who has felt a small hand slipped trustingly into hers, and has looked into an upturned, smiling face (even though neither one understands the language of the other) has seen a vision of the future of the Christian Church in Sierra Leone.

Children in the Nursery Church School

School boys working on the nursery barrie

Note the "boss" in the picture above.

The Sandbox

A young mother

See-Saw

Morlai and Phillip play with the lorry

21

Children's Church

One of the children's favorite things was the Children's Choir. We even had "robes" (white surplices) for them, and they very proudly sang in some of the church services. Each Christmas we had a Christmas program for the church, using music and drama. I would mimeograph programs, and some of the children would come to my house to cut the fronts from used Christmas cards (sent to us from the U.S.), and paste them on the front.

Children's Choir 1955

Working on programs for
Christmas service

I felt that even though the children had little, they needed to learn that Christmas was a time for sharing. So, for a few Sundays before Christmas each year the teacher would tell the children a story about children who needed help, and they would choose where their money should go. In different years we sent to our mission hospital in Nigeria, to treat a child with tuberculosis; a school for the blind in Tanzania and one in Sierra Leone; to Hong Kong for Sunday schools and nursery schools for orphan children, and to a village for orphans in Sierra Leone. For these projects we took an offering at our Christmas program. To earn money for the offering they were to do jobs for which people would pay them a little. This was similar to a program for Boy Scouts, called "bob-a-job" (A "bob" is a slang word for a shilling in England.)

And so, the children enthusiastically began work on their project. Of course, we spoke to the adult church members and asked that they give children jobs to do and pay them, as we missionaries

did also. And so the children brushed (cut) grass, gathered wood and sold it, carried water from the spring, went on errands, swept yards, and did many things to earn money. Once, as a group of children was working hard in my back yard, I heard one of the girls say, "We're not going to 'eat' this copper (use this money for themselves); this is God's work we are doing."

Finally the night came when the boys and girls were to have their Christmas program in the "big" church. Some of the children were dressed as Wise Men and shepherds; there was a Joseph and a Mary, and we had a real baby for baby Jesus. The children in the choir wore their choir robes, and sang Christmas songs they had learned. Then the time came for the offering, to which the children and the adults all contributed. Though the money was small, it was very important. One year they wrote a story about us in the Freetown newspaper. When we received letters from the places where the money had been sent, they were shared with the children.

When I returned to Rotifunk for a brief visit in 1986, I went to greet the Chief–the son of the man who had been Chief when I lived there. When I met him, he said, "Oh, yes, I remember you, Miss Megill! I remember when we had "bob-a-job" for Christmas."

And Other Activities

I also found other interesting things to do. During this time I was studying Mende with one of the teachers (though I had a problem getting anyone to come regularly). I had begun with Mende in London, because I had been told that Mende was spoken at Rotifunk. However, I discovered on arrival that Temne was the dominant language, although, as stated earlier, there were several languages spoken in the village and more in the hospital. Because the people I worked with spoke English, I did not make much progress with Mende, but it did help me to understand better the culture of the people.

Once a week for a time I taught chemistry to our dispenser, and for a time helped Bassie Kroma, a helper who worked in our house, with reading. He came to Dr. Silver an illiterate Muslim, and after five years was a sincere Christian and literate both in Temne and English. Dr. Silver had hired a teacher to teach him at first. Of course, he still had much to learn in English, and I was glad to help him because he was so eager to learn. In later years, after the hospital was turned over to the government, Bassie was able to work in the hospital. Unfortunately, I have been unable to find out whether he survived the civil war in Sierra Leone.

I also at one time taught a course in simple parasitology to our nurses and lab workers in training. During the years I trained five young men as laboratory assistants. Morlai Turay was my worker during the years, who was in charge when I was on furlough or vacation; others went to government hospitals or to one of our clinics. (More about that later.)

There were so many school children interested in looking through the microscope that I finally arranged with their science teacher to bring them over in groups. So for a time each Wednesday at 4:30 I had a group of children to whom I showed some of the things through the microscope that I saw every day. That made much more of an impression on them, I am sure, than just warning them about washing hands and food and boiling drinking water.

On Tuesday nights for one hour we had a "library hour," when school children came just to read books. They came in, took a book, and we didn't hear a thing out of anyone until we told them it was time to go home. They were so eager for reading material.

In 1951, after Dr. Smith arrived, we started a fellowship meeting on Tuesday nights for the young people of the church. It included school teachers, nurses, and some other younger people in the village. We had an average of about 18 or 20 at a time as long as we were able to have it. Winnie taught them some American fun songs and games, which everyone seemed to enjoy greatly. During one Christmas season I played some of my Christmas records and told about Christmas customs in other countries. After discussing the problem of malaria the group decided as a work project to make mosquito nets for the hospital. So for several weeks we worked on that. The meeting was always closed with a short devotional period.

Very soon after arriving in Rotifunk I felt that I could help the doctor and nurse by taking care of other matters. So, I became the one in charge of housekeeping, supervising the yard men, and doing the bookkeeping for the hospital. (I had never had training in accounting, and this was in pounds, shillings, and pence!) After only three months I was even checking out supplies for the builders of the new mission house. As the years went by I began to get up early in the morning when it was cooler and before work at the hospital to write Christian education materials. And so life at Rotifunk was very busy, sometimes difficult, but mostly interesting and challenging.

Village Life

Building a House

Frame made of sticks tied together; palm leaf roof

Putting mud balls between the sticks

"Rubbing" the house with colored and white clay

A house made from mud and wattle (sticks)

Sweeping

Carrying Wood

Pounding and Cooking Rice

Eating Rice

Washing Dishes

Making Baskets (Blys)

Making Baskets and Tie-Dyeing Cloth

Spinning Cotton

Weaving

Studying the Koran

Brushing (clearing the ground for planting)

Planting (Dryland) Rice

Planting Swamp Rice

Harvesting Rice

Threshing Rice

Drying Rice

Fanning or Winnowing Rice

Picking Cassava Leaves

Digging Sweet Potatoes

Picking Pawpaws (Papaya)

The Rains Have Come!

Collecting Palm Wine

Selling Palm Wine at the Railroad Station

The Blacksmith

Pulling a Canoe to the River (singing as they go)

Drumming and Dancing

Telling Stories Around the Fire

Chapter IV. Celebrations and Special Events

Cherish all your happy moments: they make a fine cushion for old age
–Christopher Morley (1890-1957)

There was not only work, but interesting times to learn more about life in Sierra Leone and to celebrate with friends. One afternoon my friend Honoria Bailor came over and showed me how to cook rice and stew the native way in a pot on three stones over a wood fire in the yard. Another time she showed me how to make groundnut (peanut) stew.

Ramadan

Each year the Muslims celebrate Ramadan. This is the month that Muslims devote to fasting. During daylight hours they do not eat or drink. To climax it, they have a Day of Prayer. In Rotifunk, several nights previous to that, the whole village was out dancing, drumming and singing the entire night. On two different nights Honoria took me to the place of prayer to watch them pray, and then we watched the dances and parades through the streets. They carried brightly lighted lanterns of elaborate design and colors as they went. It was beautiful and interesting to watch, but it ceased to be quite so interesting when one went to bed and tried to sleep with all the noise right outside the door!

On the Day of Prayer we went over for a few minutes in the morning to the open space where they came to pray, and I had an opportunity to take some photos. There were several of the mission school children there, and I recognized one of our Children's Church boys. I wondered as I stood there which of us would have the greater influence on them.

A float representing the train (Sierra Leone Railway)

Muslims at Prayer

A Wedding

During that month, too (in1951), I saw my first African Christian wedding. It was our head nurse who was married, and so we closed the clinic in time to go to the wedding. Weddings are quite elaborate affairs (patterned in many ways after a British church wedding), with hymns, sermon, and the ceremony. Afterward we went to the reception at the home of the bride. As we came out of the door, the "mammies" were waiting with skirts outspread to be thrown pennies or other "dashes." One had a bottle of water and wires, and offered to give "shooks" (injections), since the girl was a nurse! If she had been a teacher, someone would have had books and pencils. Before entering the door of the home, the guardian of the girl, who happened to be our minister's wife, and the girl's real mother went through a ceremony of giving water to drink, first to the bride and then to the groom, as they welcomed them to the home. Then there was a long ceremony of toasts and cutting of the cake and drinking of the "wine" (various flavors of warm soda water–since E.U.B.'s do not officially drink wine). In some cases the celebration would have lasted on into the night, with dancing and singing–perhaps for two or three nights–but since this couple were going to their new home in Freetown, it ended by escorting them to the train.

Julia Bailor and Ira Caulker Wedding

The celebration really began the night before with "Bachelor's Night." I was on the "front seat" for this entertainment, too. All the men were gathered in the house where the bridegroom was staying (who, incidentally, was not seen all night), and the women gathered in the bride's home. Then the group of men came to the door of the house where the women were, and a spokesman knocked on the door and asked for admittance. A spokesman (a man) appointed by the women demanded to know who they were, friend or enemy, and after some time were "persuaded" to let the group into the house, after they said they were looking for a "rose." They were then shown two or three women (old grannies or married women), who, they said, were not the rose they were seeking. The ceremony lasted for some time until the bride was produced and the "rose" was found. Then there was singing and dancing. Soon a calabash* containing numerous small gifts and wrapped in a colorful head scarf was presented to the bride through her spokesman, and she returned it filled with other small gifts for the groom's party. Refreshments of bread and butter were served, and then we left as the dancing and singing continued through the night.

On the day of the wedding Honoria persuaded me to wear the native dress, a "buba" and a "lappa" just like one of hers which she had given me. I am sure that I attracted more attention than the bride! But the people were very pleased, and I was the talk of the town. My friend even had a letter from Freetown commenting on it. (In later years I frequently wore bubas and lappas, gowns, or Creole print dresses.)

A River Trip

In May of 1952 some of us made a trip down the Bumpe River by launch to celebrate birthdays. Elaine, Florence, and Honoria all had birthdays in May; somehow my February birthday was always celebrated in May too. Winnie Smith was with us also. We ate rice on the way there, and salad and bread on the way back–plenty of good food. We stopped at three villages, some very small, and were shown around at each place. Everywhere we went, we were greeted in the native fashion with gifts; by the time we reached home we had about a dozen chickens, three dozen eggs, four pineapples, a bushel of rice, and about $5.50 in money. They all offered to cook for us, but we could stay only briefly at each place. One place, where there was a woman chief, had expected us to spend the night. It seemed that half the village came to meet us. I couldn't help but notice how many people there were with elephantiasis (for those of you who would have to consult Mr. Webster, THAT word means "A disease in which the skin becomes thick, hard, and fissured like an elephant's hide, and the part affected is enormously enlarged." It is caused by a parasite, a filaria, and can be treated if it is caught before the part of body becomes enlarged. When we had a surgeon, he removed very enlarged breasts and testicles.) That part of the country had lots of it, as well as sleeping sickness, or trypanasomiasis, also caused by a parasite. We started our trip about noon and returned at 7:00, just at dark, tired and full of food.

Scenes from the Bompe River

33

Esther L. Megill

<u>The Anglican Archbishop Visits</u>

During that year we also had the excitement of a visit from Anglican Archbishop Fisher, the Archbishop of Canterbury. He arrived on the governor's train, and stopped long enough to meet the hospital staff.

Dr. Silver greets Archbishop Fisher

The Archbishop greets staff members

<u>Coronation of Queen Elizabeth</u>

On June 2, 1953 the whole country celebrated the Coronation of Queen Elizabeth II. I went to Moyamba for that event. We listened to the ceremony as it was broadcast on the radio. (We had no radio at Rotifunk.)

The Rotifunk Celebration

Bundu* Girls Ready for the Celebration

Drummers and Dancers

"Devil" Dancer

Snake Charmer

Vacation in Shenge

In January of 1952 I started on a long looked-forward-to vacation to Shenge. This time I did not stay in the mission house, but with Honoria in her mother's home. Honoria had a new baby (Mervin), and he helped to keep us entertained and busy. We started from Rotifunk by launch at about 5:30 p.m. on January 22. The time of starting always depended upon the tide, for it was a tidal river. We had part of the journey by open sea, and because of the fog, we got lost. When the men discovered that we were past Shenge, they just dropped anchor and waited until sunrise. I did not enjoy that very much, for I easily get seasick on a rolling ocean. At 7:00 we started again, and arrived back in Shenge at 9:30, where we were welcomed by Mrs. Priscilla Caulker (Honoria's mother), in whose home we were staying. Then followed twenty-one days of the most delightful and restful vacation that I had ever had. We slept and ate, and ate and slept. Then after a few days I had the energy to go visiting with her, and we went swimming and fishing in the ocean (but no fish, worse luck!) It was so nice to never be in a hurry about anything and to go to bed any time we liked–even if it was after breakfast (or tea, as the Africans called it). I ate almost entirely African food, though Honoria served me rice only once a day, knowing that Americans like variety. And she went without much pepper on her food for my sake. We had "tea" when we got up, which consisted of tea or coffee, bread, or perhaps plantains. She served me eggs, too, fixed in a most delicious way with onions and

The Shenge Launch

Mrs. Priscilla Caulker

a little bit of African pepper. We had all the grapefruit, oranges, and bananas we could eat–and I had a whole pineapple to myself on a number of days. At anywhere from 1:30-2:30 we had rice, with stew, sauce, or pepper soup. Stew is made with palm oil, coconut oil, or groundnut oil, onions, tomato paste, and meat–chicken or fish (fish is much preferred, and much more common in Shenge)–and, of course, plenty of pepper. Sauce is made the same way, only green (sweet) potato leaves or cassava or other leaves are added. Pepper soup is made without the oil. The stew or the soup is served over the rice. Rice and stew, sauce, or soup is the staple food of the Sierra Leoneans and is eaten at least once a day–more, if it is available. At 7:30-9:00 o'clock, we would have yams, cassava, or plantains with stew, tea or coffee, and bread–again, with any fruit we wanted. I practiced eating with my hand the African way (and it is an art!) and really enjoyed it.

One day I took Honoria and two of her cousins, Lucy and Ellen Caulker, both teachers in the local (mission) school, on an American weiner roast (with canned frankfurters), though they were a little dubious about eating hot <u>dogs</u>! They agreed they were "sweet" (good) though.

Houses in villages in Sierra Leone are made with a stick framework, the sticks being tied together with vines or rope made from palm leaves, then the spaces filled with mud. A final smooth coat is rubbed on, and then usually covered with clay, most often white, and often with designs in other colors. The roof is made from bamboo and thatched with grass, or with folded palm or bamboo leaves. As people were able, they built houses with mud bricks (or even concrete, especially in the larger towns and cities), and had "pan" roofs made from aluminum (aluminium to

the British and Sierra Leoneans) or steel. The houses in that part of Sierra Leone are usually square or rectangular, though some areas in the north have the round houses which many people think are found everywhere in Africa. [See the photos on p.25.]

On one evening some of the school boys came to dance for me. Drumming and dancing are the chief entertainments–and singing always goes along with it. That evening, the boys did dances and skipped rope to the rhythm of the drums. That night they had only one rope, but they were so skillful and graceful in jumping that I was fascinated. I was told, however, that sometimes they have as many as eight or nine ropes going at once.

On two other evenings children came to tell stories to me. They spoke in Sherbro, and Honoria interpreted into English. They told African folk stories and fables, some of which I wrote down as they told them. This is another favorite form of entertainment among the Africans. They sometimes go on all night, seeing who can tell the most stories.

On one day we took a long walk overland to "The Point," a point of land jutting out into the sea. We passed through several small villages on the way, and stopped many times to greet friends and relatives of Honoria and her cousins who were with me. I often heard remarks about my "open" teeth. The African is quite expressive and never hesitates to say what he thinks about another person, especially when he knows (or thinks) we don't understand. But I had an interpreter with me this time. I soon learned the words, though, so I became quite embarrassed when people started talking. One woman said that I didn't have teeth like a white man (person)—they were quite beautiful!

After we reached our destination, we rested on the seashore in the shade of a palm tree and ate oranges and coconuts. Then we walked back barefooted along the beach—and were really ready for our rice and a nap when we got home

Esther Megill, Honoria Bailor, Lucy Caulker

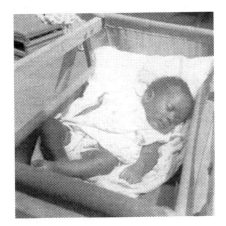

Kenneth Mervin Bailor, Shenge, January 1952

A Missionary Wedding

There were also two weddings of missionaries in the years I was in Sierra Leone. In August of 1951 we welcomed Dr. Winifred Smith to our staff. Winnie, Ethel Brooks, and I had all been classmates at York College. On December 21, 1952, her fiancee, Lester Bradford, arrived in Sierra Leone, just in time for their wedding at Rotifunk on Dec. 23. Ethel Brooks and a new missionary at Harford School, Anne Fitchner, arrived with Les on the train on Monday, the 22nd. That night we had the wedding dinner, with twenty-two people present. You can imagine the work it took to get ready in two days to feed and lodge twenty-two people! Many of the missionaries were able to come. The big wedding was on Tuesday, at 10:00 a.m. The bride wore the usual white dress with a train; I was the maid-of-honor (or chief bridesmaid, as they are called in Sierra Leone). Ethel Brooks and Carolyn Temple (daughter of Paul and Marianne) were also bridesmaids. We all wore just what we had or could borrow, but did manage to all have dotted Swiss formals—mine, blue, and the others, pink, and pearls. The best man was Paul Temple; Les Shirley gave away the bride; the four men on our hospital staff were ushers; and Hilton, the 6-year-old son of the Bailors, was ring bearer. Marianne Temple, Grace Shirley, and Florence Barnhart sang as a trio. Lois Olsen played the pump organ. The church was crowded, for not only was it the wedding of the doctor, but also the first "white" wedding people had ever seen. Bishop Warner, who had come to Sierra Leone to hold Conference, gave the charge to the bride and groom. Dr. S. M. Renner, Sierra Leone superintendent of the Freetown District, performed the double-ring ceremony. Then Bishop Warner gave the charge which was from the commissioning service for missionaries. Rev. B. A. Carew, superintendent of the Bo District, gave communion to the bride and groom. At this point, in a usual American ceremony, we would have gone out of the church. However, we had a sermon by the Rev. T. B. Williams, pastor of the Rotifunk Church, as is the African (British) custom. From Monday night until Wednesday morning there was continual dancing, drumming, and singing. Even during the ceremony there was the sound of drumming outside. When we reached the outside some of our African friends threw rice (we had instructed them in the American custom), but we were mobbed by the singing and dancing people. The bridegroom threw pennies to the people there (another African custom), and the bride threw the bouquet (I tried hard, but Lois Olsen shoved the hardest and so caught it!).

We finally managed to get through the crowd and take a few pictures. Then there was a reception afterward, in the Sierra Leone custom, with toasts by several of the wedding party, soft drinks, cake, and plenty of rice. Afterward the bride and groom disappointed everyone (the Africans, that is) by going in the lorry to Moyamba with the Harford missionaries, and then went on the next day to Shenge for their honeymoon. (Dr. Silver had warned them that the African custom would have been to have some of the older women stay up all night until the bed sheet could be brought to them from the bridal bed, to inspect for blood. This would have shown that the bride had been a virgin, and would have been the cause of great rejoicing.)

Mr. & Mrs. Lester Bradford
Dec. 23, 1952

The Wedding Party
Carolyn Temple, Ethel Brooks, Dr. S. M. Renner, Esther Megill,
Winnie and Les Bradford,
(Hilton Bailor in front), Paul Temple (Gordon Temple? in front), ?,
Ernest Kroma, W. C. Barley

Shenge Again

I had previously planned a vacation in Shenge, and in fact had returned for the wedding, along with Honoria. We returned by launch the day of the wedding.

Some of the Shenge people worked hard cleaning up the mission house and preparing it for the newlyweds. They also kept them well supplied with food while they were there. Honoria and I showed them some of Shenge; we all went for a weiner roast on the beach, crabbing, and to Plantain Island. One morning Les Bradford and I swam to Monkey Island–I can't guess how far it was. We were disappointed in not seeing any monkeys, and came back with cuts on our legs and arms from the sharp rocks that surrounded the island, and a few jellyfish stings, but we did enjoy it–also the fresh coconuts that were waiting for us when we returned.

On Christmas Eve some of the school teachers (graduates of Harford School and Albert Academy) and present students of those schools home on vacation formed a caroling party. We walked toward the mission house beach, singing carols as we went–we had a drum also. Then we

Picnic on the Beach
Lucy Caulker, Honoria Bailor,
Ellen & Lucy Caulker

Crabbing

serenaded the Bradfords, and went to the point of land looking out over the sea in front of the mission house. There we made a fire and popped some Kansas popcorn which I had provided and ate cookies and oranges. All the time we were doing this we sang Christmas carols, and just before we left at 12:00 switched to choruses. Before we were dismissed, they asked me to lead in prayer. The Harford girls sang a carol they knew under the Bradford's window and then we went back to the town–this time, everyone but I was dancing and singing "Christmas done come, and we no die-o," (Krio). [Unfortunately in my strict upbringing I never learned to dance, and did not easily enter into the African dancing.]

We were wakened before daylight on Christmas morning with the sound of a group of people singing "While Shepherds Watched Their Flocks by Night," and "Blest Be the Tie that Binds." We went out to find a group from the Chief's compound, led by Chief Caulker himself. He had not been well for several years, and so thanked God that he was able to come greet us on Christmas morning. We followed them to one or two houses, and then went back to bed. We got up late, just in time to go to the morning church service. There was dancing and singing all through the town, for there can be no celebration in Africa without it. The children in the house in which we stayed were out most of the day with their "devil" mask (they took turns wearing it), and beating on bottles and cans with sticks as they sang and danced. As they went from house to house people would give them money. That is also the custom when groups of adults come around. There is always plenty of rice to eat on Christmas, too, of course. They do not ordinarily give gifts as we do, although they share special food with friends. The day before Christmas I had some of the children help me cut a tree (there were no evergreens), put it in a bucket of sand, and make decorations for it from construction paper and aluminum foil. They were quite pleased with it. I had brought small gifts for everyone there, and so when they were wrapped in Christmas paper and put under the tree it seemed like Christmas to me, too. That night they opened the gifts, to climax my African-American Christmas.

The "Kangalii" Devil Dancer

Children with Christmas
Devil Dancer

Child with a "Devil" Mask; our Christmas Tree

Honoria with Chief A. T. Caulker

Weiner Roast
Lucy & Ellen Caulker, Honoria Bailor

The day after Christmas is "Boxing Day" according to English custom, so the dancing continued–in fact, some people still danced until the New Year's. The Bradfords returned to Rotifunk on December 31 by launch, but met with some bad luck. There was a storm at sea, and most of their belongings were washed overboard, including film with the photographs they had taken. Fortunately, no one was hurt.

As mentioned earlier, one of the places we took the Bradfords was to Plantain Island, an island just off Shenge. There are many fishermen there, and one sees the fish being smoked, to be sent up-country for sale. Fishermen were mending nets, some were going out or coming in in canoes with their catch. It is a small island, and we easily walked around it. On the way we saw a tree with pieces of white cloth tied on it. It was explained to us that some people thought there were spirits in the tree. As we walked along, we discovered an old canon, half buried in the sand. Upon examining it more closely, we noticed the engraved crest of King George III of England. This was before the time the British established the Sierra Leone Colony, but British ships were coming to Plantain Island and the shores of Sierra Leone to collect black men and women, to be carried to the Americas and sold as slaves. In fact, the canon was on one of those slave ships, perhaps even the one belonging to John Newton.

At the end of the island we found further evidence of the blight of the slave trade. Some of the stone walls were still standing. They had made a slave pen, where John Newton collected the captives from the mainland until enough were gathered to put aboard a slaving ship. Honoria said, "This is where they kept my people until they could be sent to America and sold as slaves."Whenever I sing one of the hymns written by John Newton (the most familiar being "Amazing Grace") I see that scene and hear Honoria's words.

Scenes at Plantain Island

Fishing Boats

Honoria and Esther at Remains of Newton's Slave Pen

Mending a Net

Drying Fish (Bonga)

Other Scenes in Shenge

Making a Canoe–Shenge

Sembehun to Shenge Road–Making a Canoe

The House Where Honoria Was Born

New Home–Honoria's First Home-

Castor Bean Plant

Breadfruit Tree

Honoria, Elaine Gasser, Florence Barnhart,
Tennyson Caulker

Pineapples!

Collecting Seaweed

Honoria and Esther Washing Rice

Honoria and Esther
1955

Vacation time! The two Esthers–Esther Megill and Esther Bailor

Grating and Cutting Cassava

And Another Wedding

It was several years later, on January 1, 1957, that the missionary family attended another wedding of two of its members. The Rev. Clyde Galow and Gladys Fahner, a nurse-midwife at Taiama, were married in the Calvary Church in Taiama. This beautiful church was called "The Cathedral in the Bush," and was built when the Rev. B. A. Carew was pastor. The Rev. Charles Leader was the officiating minister, Lois Olsen the organist. The Matron of Honor was Joy Thede; Groomsmen, Jack Thomas and Franklin Kongo; Maid of Honor, Musu Morsay; and ushers, seven graduates of the Bo Bible Training School where Clyde was stationed (and Gladys also, after the wedding). Hymns were sung and communion was given. A luncheon was served in the Native Administration Court Barrie after the service. The missionaries had a shower for them of canned goods–from which we had removed the labels!

Clyde & Gladys Galow, U.S.,1958

45

Jeep Trails and Dirt Roads

Three days after the wedding three of the Harford School teachers (Florence Barnhart, Elaine Gasser, and Lucile Esbenshade) and I started on an adventurous trip through French Guinea and Liberia. We drove the Harford jeep station wagon. Our adventures filled pages, which we produced upon our return, in a booklet called "Jeep Trails and Dirt Roads." In spite of all that happened along the way (almost impassable roads, two nights in the bush, a bent tie-rod, brakes gone, clutch gone, and leaking oil, all at various times), we always found help when it was needed. We met many wonderful people. Some of them spoke no English at all, but fortunately Florence remembered enough of her high school and college French to help us out, along with sign language! Some of the missionaries we met were Methodist, whom I learned to know well in later years when we were all United Methodists.

Liberian Road

Meals by the Roadside:
Florence Barnhart, Esther Megill, Lucile Esbenshade

The New Capitol, Monrovia

The Trip to Kono

There were other trips, too. In February of 1961 Lois Olsen (midwife at Taiama) Marjorie Hager (bookkeeper at Harford), Betty Carew (wife of our pastor at Taiama), and I took a ten-day trip up to Kono. This was the first opportunity I had had in all the years I had been there to see Kono (other than a quick trip to collect Ruth Harding's things when we had to send her home), so I was glad for a chance to go. Highlights of the trip were visits to Union Teacher Training College at Bunumbu, in which the E.U.B. Church cooperated; the Methodist Hospital (British) at Segbwema; our mission at Jaiama; a hike over to the falls at Jaiama Nimiyama, which was well worth the effort; a conducted tour of the Sierra Leone Selection Trust (S.L.S.T.) Diamond

Esther Megill, Lois Olsen, Betty Carew, Marj Hager

mines; a visit to the new mosque at Koidu, where we took off our shoes to go inside; and a visit with the Thomas's at our newest mission station at Yekeior.

Scenes in Kono

Koidu

Koidu Mosque

The Tower of the Mosque from which the Call to Prayer is Given

Climbing to Falls at Jaiama Nimiyama

Looking Down on the Falls

Marj Hager, Lois Olsen, Sahrfili Matturi at Falls

Yengema Diamond Mines

S.L.S.T. Training Center

Digging for Diamonds

Transporting diamond-bearing soil to the Concentration Plant (above)

Diamond-bearing dirt mixed with water

Sludge poured over greased conveyer belts

Grease is scraped off, heated, and the diamonds picked out

Jaiama

Jaiama Clinic and Maternity Center (E.U.B.)

Women Waiting for Clinic

Jaiama Secondary School
(E.U.B.)

Yekeier

House Under Construction

Dolores Thomas's Clinic (Yekeier)

Bundu Girl*

Blacksmith

Making Palm Oil

After cutting the bunches of palm kernels from the tree, they are fermented for about three days, then pounded in a mortar until the fibers are removed. They are then removed from the mortar and mixed with water (in this scene from Kono, the woman is mixing them by stomping on them). The nuts and fibers are then removed, and the oil skimmed off the water. This is then heated slowly until all the water is removed, the oil cooled, and put into bottles.

(I observed a somewhat different method of obtaining palm oil in Shenge. Palm oil is a very common ingredient in making the stew or sauce used on rice.)

Scene at the River

Weaver

A Place of Sacrifice

Second Trip to Liberia

Roadside Cafe–Jill, Audrey, Lois

A short time before I left Sierra Leone in 1962, I made another trip to Liberia, this time with Lois Olsen and two British women from Njala. I remember that as we discussed what we could take to eat along the way (there were no restaurants or motels in Sierra Leone and Liberia), I suggested we could take eggs, and boil them. (We had a small kerosene burner on which we could cook.) One of the British women said, "But how can we eat them with no egg cups?" Of course we two Americans assured them that we had never used egg cups until we went to England, and we would show them how to do it!

We drove to Bo and Kenema, then to Kambia at the easternmost end of Sierra Leone. The first night we stopped at a government rest house where we camped out, using the bedding we had brought with us. The market at Kambia was a large one, and interesting. At the Liberian border we had a problem with the soldier there. He kept insisting that we had to have papers stamped in Monrovia (which, of course, we would not reach until the end of our trip). Eventually however, he allowed us to pass into Liberia. We traveled on a dirt, but well-kept road, through sparsely settled and cultivated territory, with towering trees and thick bush on either side . The next night we stayed at a small mission station, with an acquaintance of mine, and then drove on to Monrovia. There we stayed at the Lutheran guest house. We had planned to explore Monrovia the next day, but discovered it was a national holiday. Everything was closed, and there was a big parade. That afternoon we did visit the government buildings, some of which were open, and drove out to the port. It was a "free port" and attracted a great deal of international trade. At the port we discovered the car battery was dead, but an American man took it and recharged it.

On the way to Monrovia we had passed through the Firestone Rubber Plantation. There we were able to take photographs of various stages in the production of rubber and getting it ready to ship to the States. We also stopped at the Methodist Hospital in Ganta (later this became familiar to me), and the Lutheran Hospital at Zorzor, also run by American missionaries.[6]

Entering Liberia

Monrovia, from Fifth Floor of the Ducor Hotel

The Rubber Plantation

Rubber Trees

Tapping the tree for sap

Delivering latex (sap) to the processing plant

Chemicals are added to cause the latex to coagulate

Coagulated latex is rolled into sheets
of crepe rubber

After drying, the rubber is pressed into bales, and
marked with the grade of rubber. They are now ready
to ship to the United States.

Ganta Methodist Mission

Woodcarvers (leprosy patients)
outside Ganta Hospital

Other Holidays

I also had vacations with other missionaries at Hamilton Beach near Freetown, and at Leicester, a rest house on a hill above Freetown where it was cooler. We usually spent Christmas with other missionaries, often at Moyamba. Each year we met in a missionary retreat, which was a great deal of fun as well as inspirational. In the early years we all went to Annual Conference, too, and although there were meetings and business to take care of, we enjoyed the companionship. As Conference leadership developed, we missionaries attended only when we were on a Conference committee.

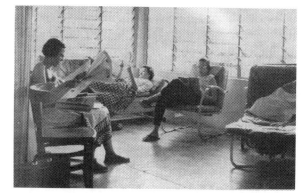

Vacation at Hamilton Beach, August 1960
Lois Lehman, Elaine Gasser, Donna Colbert

View from the Rest House

These vacations and times together were good, but I have always been grateful that I was able to stay in Honoria's home, for she taught me so much about Sierra Leone life and culture. I was told that the people appreciated the fact that I would stay in an African home also. In Shenge I was known as "Cousin Esther," and Honoria and her children and grandchildren called me "Auntie Esther." (And her children and grandchildren still do.)

Chapter V. Trouble in Sierra Leone

Sierra Leone had seemed to be a peaceful country, but in early 1955 there was unrest. All the day laborers went on strike in Freetown, and it quickly turned into mob rule. Dozens of people were killed and others wounded; electric wires were torn down, water pipes torn up, and much damage done to shops and homes, particularly of the Lebanese and Syrians. Twenty-four European families and several Syrian/Lebanese families were actually hiding in the army barracks during those days. We, of course, received nothing from Freetown, including mail, and no trains ran for several days. The army had to take over and a strict curfew imposed. Negotiations about wages continued and there was a trial of some of the offenders. In Rotifunk, however, we were not at all worried or afraid during this difficult time in Freetown.

Times were hard for many people, for the cost of living had soared. A bushel of rice actually cost three times as much when I returned from furlough in December 7, 1954 as it had the year before when I left. The country was importing rice from Italy.

> It was a strange Christmas and New Year's in Rotifunk that year.

One of the main problems was that the population was going wild over the illicit diamond business, for diamonds were being discovered in other places in the country besides in the area where mines were already operating. The laws, though strict, were flagrantly disobeyed. Everyone wanted to get rich quickly with diamonds instead of doing the hard work of farming. And, unfortunately, there was too much of the idea that an educated man doesn't work with his hands. There were some good signs, however; for instance during the previous year an agricultural demonstration center was started in Rotifunk. But there was more and more of a strong nationalistic feeling. Most of us Americans were in sympathy with the desire for freedom of government, yet we could see that in many ways the people were not yet ready for it. However, more and more responsibility was being put into the hands of the Africans, and the British government seemed to be making an effort to prepare the country for independence.

In December of that year, however, we had some excitement at Rotifunk. In the middle of the night on December 4 we were wakened by someone pounding at our door, and opened it to find that one of the local Native Administration officials was there, begging to be allowed to stay to protect himself from a mob of men. We learned then that hundreds of men with clubs were marching, singing and shouting, through the town, destroying the homes of all those connected with collecting taxes and threatening to kill the officials or run them out of town. We told our friend that he could stay until the goods (freight) train came in bound for Freetown, and then he must run down the hill from our house and get on it. This he did. (Later, when it was all over, a man told me, "We knew he was in there, and if he had not left we would have come get him.") Some terrified women and children began to come to the hospital and our house for shelter. Needless to say, there was little sleep for the rest of the night. All around us we saw the light of burning buildings and heard the sound of gun powder being set off (there were no guns). We could hear the rather chilling Poro* yell. The "reign of terror" lasted off and on for three days. In fact, it was several weeks before people began to settle down and feel safe once again. In Rotifunk thirty houses were burned or destroyed. Our Chief was gone at the time and the rest of the government officials left during that night or the next day. There was absolutely no law except that of the mob. However, no one else was bothered except those who were in the Native Administration, although some other houses were threatened and everyone was under constant tension. I went down to the railroad station where there was a telephone–the only one in town–and called the British District Commissioner in Moyamba to ask him to send help–not for us, but for the sake of the people. He asked me, however, how we were, and reminded me that he was responsible for the welfare of expatriates. I told him that people were coming to us for help, including some wounded ones, and I did not feel we were in danger. The D.C. did come with a few soldiers on Monday morning, but left soon after. We found out afterward that the reason he didn't stay was that there were so few policemen they could have done nothing anyway, for there were disturbances in other places and houses burnt throughout the country. Finally we did get police protection in Rotifunk. There was no loss of life, but other places were not so fortunate. At no time was I afraid the mob would molest us or the mission property, for they had respect and appreciation for us. The thing that made the situation bad was the tension which everyone was under for days, and the homeless women and children. We hoped that conditions in the local government, which brought on the trouble, would be remedied, for the people really did have a just grievance in many cases. There had been much graft and corruption in connection with the collection of taxes. Also, the nonliterate people had not been educated as to the necessity for taxes for schools, hospitals, roads, etc.

It was a strange Christmas and New Year's in Rotifunk that year. For the first time there was no singing and dancing on those days, as was always the custom. People just did not feel like rejoicing.

Some of the houses which were destroyed in Rotifunk

Chapter VI. New Staff–More Medical Work

Gertrude Bloede and I had been in Rotifunk for less than two months when Dr. Silver and Ruth Harding left for a very necessary rest at the rest house at Mt. Leicester above Freetown. We surprised ourselves at how well we managed without a doctor, but were eagerly looking forward to her return. Of course Gertrude had the medical responsibility, although I did more "diagnosing" than a technologist is supposed to try to do.

Both Dr. Silver and Ruth came back soon, but Ruth was ill, and became seriously so. In May Dr. Silver took Ruth to England for treatment (more about that in the next chapter). Once again we were alone, until Dr. Winifred Smith (mentioned earlier) arrived in August of that year.

Gertrude Bloede,
Esther Megill,
Winifred Smith,
wearing Creole prints
and Rotifunk hats

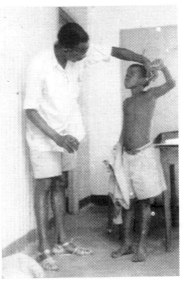

Alfred Kroma and
Leprosy Patient

Alfred Kroma, whom we had sent to Nigeria for training in the diagnosis and treatment of leprosy, also returned. He started leprosy clinics, under supervision of the doctor, of course. The news spread so far that in less than a year's time he had 171 leprosy patients registered for treatment. By 1953 there were 1,100 different patients treated, and clinics were held four times a week.

A long series of treatment is necessary, but the improvement is marked if the medicine is taken regularly. At that time the treatment was new, and it was not known whether the disease was really cured or just arrested. Now they know that it can be cured. Also, if children who live in a home where persons have leprosy are treated, they can be prevented from getting it. Unfortunately, there were many people who came with advanced stages of the disease and little could be done for them.

Winnnie had been in Rotifunk only a few weeks when a man was brought in who had been beaten by thieves, and she did emergency surgery on him. So I suddenly became an anesthetist and gave the ether, while Gertrude scrubbed as nurse. Ernest, our dresser, also assisted. There was a mad scramble to hunt up all the surgical instruments which had not been used since Dr. Smart, our Sierra Leone doctor, had left some years before. We dumped them in to be boiled, and prepared a few at least semi-sterile things. This was what one could really call "public medicine!" The office has nice big windows, and whenever anything interesting was happening, a crowd soon gathered on all sides. So we were watched the entire time. It began to get dark as the operation progressed, and it had to be finished by lamp light and flashlight.

In 1952 Dr. Smith arranged with a drug company to allow us to use an experimental drug to treat tuberculosis, since we had no other treatment. Tuberculosis was one of the scourges of the country. Day after day we saw people who had it, and for which nothing could be done. The people have so little resistance to it (since it was brought to Africa by Europeans), and it spreads rapidly because of the living conditions and ignorance about how it is spread. We had enough to try on eight people. You might think that we would be flooded with requests for treatment, but instead we had to plead and argue to get the people to try it. We admitted three patients at first. One was a teacher from Freetown–she was educated and understood just what having tuberculosis meant. The other two were nonliterate people, a man and a woman with a small baby. The use of the drug meant regular laboratory tests on patients, for we had to keep careful records and report results to the pharmaceutical company. Because we had no x-ray we had to send the patients to Freetown for a chest x-ray before we admitted them, and another at the end of the treatment.

The new drug–or a combination of drugs–did prove successful, and even after Dr. Smith left after her marriage, we continued to treat patients. Two of them were children–Fattu and James, whom we learned to love. They were both in the hospital for some weeks for treatment, and then had to come once a month for medicine. They were both about six or seven years old. You can imagine that we quite spoiled them while they were in the hospital. James was in the longest (he felt quite lost after Fattu left.) He got into trouble a few times, too. Once he "tiefed" (stole) some dried fish from another patient. The evidence, in the form of a few fish bones, was found in his bed while he slept away with an angelic look on his face. At another time, he and Fattu stole some meat from the cooking pot of another patient. In a way, we could not blame them, for they, especially James, really did not have enough to eat. (Family members had to prepare food and feed our inpatients.) When we discovered that James was being brought food by his family only once a day, and then sometimes not until eight or nine o'clock at night, we began to take him food. It is true that many, many children in Sierra Leone eat only once a day, but for a tuberculosis patient, it is particularly important that they have plenty of good, wholesome food. The worst punishment for James and Fattu was to be made to stay in bed. When James stole the fish, he had to stay in bed the whole afternoon, in spite of his tears. When one of the nurses asked him why he didn't stay in bed more so that he would be well more quickly, he answered, "Stay in bed? Why should I stay in bed? When I am up, I can find mangoes and guavas to eat!" As you can see, our hospital was run in a fashion that would shock anyone in the United States!

James, like most African children, was willing to share whatever he had. Once I gave him a penny to buy something to eat. He came back with two pancakes (with hot pepper sauce) and offered one to me! At another time, he borrowed my knife to cut an avocado, and then gave me half. He was rather upset when I at first tried to make him keep it to eat, but when I saw that he really wanted me to accept it, and did, he was all smiles. At another time (these things happened after he was discharged from the hospital), he came in with a proud smile and the announcement, "I send this for you." (They say that even when they bring something themselves.) Inside a piece of cloth was one small catfish, a crab, and a number of small water creatures of various descriptions which he had caught in the river. Though the contents did not particularly appeal to me, I took them with real gratefulness, for I knew that he had given what he had to say "thank you." James was much better. His hair, which was straight when he was so ill, was nice and curly again. He looked well. I do not know whether his family had him take his pills regularly and whether he did fully recover.

Dr. Silver returned in early 1952. There was a time, when Gertrude went home for a well-deserved furlough, that Dr. Silver and I were the only missionaries on the staff at Rotifunk. Then came Dr. Silver's illness (see the next chapter). In 1953 an English nurse-midwife, Betty Beveridge, came to start a midwifery training school. She was ill for months, again a disease that was never diagnosed. (See next chapter). During that time Lois Olsen was ordered to come to Rotifunk, which she really didn't want to do, for she was busy with her own work at Taiama, and was here for a time. Then we had a Sierra Leonean-trained nurse from Freetown for a short time. In 1955 Metra Heisler finished her midwifery training in England, and was assigned to Rotifunk. In April of 1956 we were joined by Dr. Al French, his wife Barbara and their two children. (He did not stay with us long.) In 1956 we were glad to welcome Dr. George Harris, his wife Norma, and their children. In 1957 Dr. Lowell Gess and family arrived. His wife, Ruth, was a nurse also. Dr. Gess was a surgeon, so our surgery was now kept busy. We had some new houses built for residences before they arrived. Dr. Stephenson and his family joined us late in 1961. Gertrude Bloede and Metra Heisler were at times assigned to Jaiama or Taiama, depending on which midwife was on furlough, but they were at Rotifunk many of the years they were in Sierra Leone.

Betty Beveridge at a Village Clinic

Esther Megill and Metra Heisler

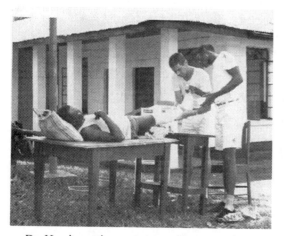

Dr. Harris putting a cast on a leprosy patient

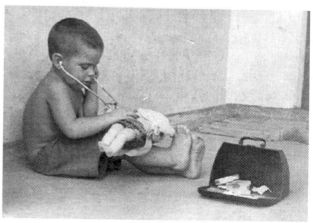

Young Dr. (Andy) Harris

Betty Beveridge started a Midwifery training school, which increased our staff and also helped to provide staff to other clinics.

Hospital Staff 1960

<u>Back, L. to R.:</u> Moses Butcher, Matthew Kamara, Alfred Kroma, James Fallah, Joseph Cole (Kamara), Julius Caulker, Samuel Bendu, Edwin Lavaly, Maxwell Carew.

<u>Middle Row:</u> Julia Caulker, Mary Lavaly, Zainabu Kallon, Gladys Kandeh, Tator Bagrey, Yeabu Sesay, Marjorie Cole, Lois Short, Emma Kagbo, Nana Turay, Abigail Johnson, Nancy Judy.

<u>Absent:</u> David Johnson, Juliana Will, Marian Caulker

<u>Missionaries:</u> Lowell A. Gess, M.D.; Esther Megill, M.T. (A.S.C.P.); Betty Beveridge, S.R.N., S.C.M.; Mabel I. Silver, M.D.; Gertrude Bloede, R.N., S.C.M.; George Harris, M.D.

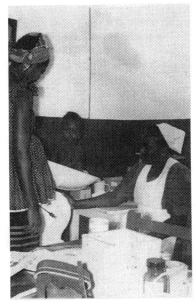

Midwife Abigail Johnson, Baby Clinic

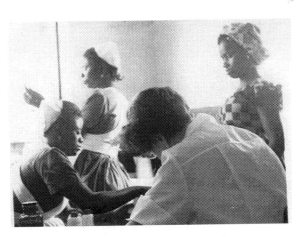

Betty Beveridge, Prenatal Clinic

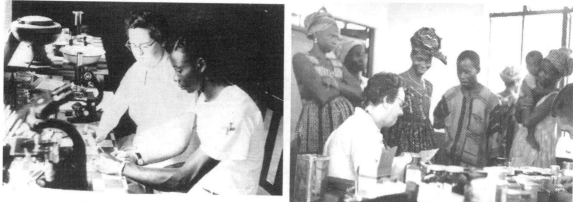

Esther Megill with Morlai
Turay, Lab Assistant

Dr. Silver at work

In late 1955 and 1956 there was a smallpox epidemic in many parts of Sierra Leone, and so we had one to four patients in the hospital for some months. It was really impossible to keep them isolated, though we tried. Vaccination campaigns were carried on everywhere, but it was very

difficult to reach all the people. Many of them hid cases of smallpox, or ran away when they heard someone had come to vaccinate them. On the other hand, we also had people frequently come to ask for "maculate," as they called it. Some years later WHO carried on an extensive campaign, and now there is no smallpox anywhere in the world, except for a few organisms being kept in a laboratory somewhere. Another disease which was conquered was yaws. After penicillin was discovered and became plentiful, WHO had a campaign, and conquered that disease. It was caused by an organism, a spirochete, similar to the syphilis organism, although it was not a sexually transmitted disease.

During one of the times when Dr. Silver was gone and Betty

Smallpox vaccination
Ernest Kroma
Metra Heisler

Beveridge was left in charge of the medical work, I made a discovery in the laboratory that I will never forget. Honoria Bailor brought in her baby–her only girl, named after me–because she was ill. Miss Beveridge asked me to check her for malaria, and when I pricked her finger to get blood, I realized that the child was very anemic. We knew that Honoria took good care of her children, and so the first thought that came to my mind was sickle cell anemia. I went to Betty and told her that Esther was very anemic. She looked at me and said, "Check her for sickle cell anemia."

We had a very simple procedure that I could do in the lab. After preparing the drop of blood so that there was little access to air, I looked in the microscope-and immediately saw the peculiar sickle-shaped cells that are characteristic of the anemia. Honoria was sitting there with the baby, and I am sure she knew something was wrong. Tears came to my eyes, and I went in to tell Betty the results of the test. She said, "Tell her to send for Teacher Bailor." (He was Headmaster of the nearby school.)

Esther Bailor,
1956

I returned and told Honoria, and she sent for him. When he came, Betty took them into the small examination room, and told them that Esther had sickle cell anemia. She also warned them that any other children might also have the disease. It was a sad time, and there is still no cure for the disease, but Esther is still well most of the time and is presently working as a CNA (Certified Nursing Assistant) in the U.S. She had been a refugee in Guinea with her mother, and later was able to come with her two children to join her husband, who had been in the States for some time.[7]

When Dr. Silver returned and learned of the diagnosis, she realized that the death of Honoria's first child, a boy, had been due to sickle cell anemia. A later child also has the disease, and some of the others are carriers. Perhaps some day there will be a way to prevent the disease from developing. Research with genes is encouraging.

Early in December of 1959 a new boat, the *Bumpe Evangel*, was dedicated. The boat was used to go to villages down the Bumpe River for medical and evangelistic purposes.

Dr. Lowell Gess & Rev. W. B.
Claye, Pastor at Rotifunk

Dedication of the *Bompe Evangel*.
Posed to show work of the mobile team

It was during that year that I was able to train Morlai Turay to help me in the lab. Also, we reveled in the electricity which we had for three hours every morning, for I now had an electric centrifuge, rather than the one turned by hand, and a light for my microscope. Since the lights were also on in the evenings, I spent part of some evenings in the lab, too. We had a beautiful new microscope, direct from Germany, the best I had ever used

After the two doctors came, Dr. Harris was finally able to install the x-ray machine that had been waiting in storage for several years until we could find someone to do it. The Board had asked me during a previous furlough to take six weeks of x-ray training, which I did, in a hospital in Santa Fe, New Mexico. However, I was never able to use what little I had learned. By the time the x-ray machine was installed new solutions and film had to be ordered, and I soon left Sierra Leone.

On Christmas Eve in 1959 a terrible train wreck occurred east of Rotifunk. A train employee, who had come in the engine, ran frantically to Dr. Gess's house and took him to the scene of the accident. In his book, *Mine Eyes Have Seen the Glory*, he describes the terrible scene that he saw when he arrived. He also tells of his astonishment when he arrived home in the early hours of the morning, to be told that an injured child held in her mother's arms was lying at the door of the hospital. When they moved the child to examine her, he says "I couldn't believe my eyes. I had

67

seen this child at the wreck. When we had moved this unconscious child to examine her, the head toppled to her back. Her neck had been cut from side to side, completely severing the muscles that held the head forward and erect. I had spent no time on this hopeless condition and had moved on to the next patient."[8]

However, the doctor and his staff immediately took the child, Marie Jones, to surgery, and performed a complicated operation . . . Betty Beveridge wrote,[9] "Morning time saw Marie battered and broken, swathed in bandages, but . . . very much alive. Her mother, who had lost Marie's sister, uncle and two cousins in the accident, was still in a state of shock and could not appreciate, just yet, that Marie was going to live. Three days later, during the Sunday morning ward service, Marie, complete with bandages and trailing the tails of the long white shirt she was wearing, wandered out of the small ward where we had placed her into the main ward to join the other patients for prayers."

Betty's account continues: "Marie, in simple trust and with great courage, progressed from day to day. She must have had quite a deal of pain when her dressings were done, but she made few complaints. Eating must have been quite a problem, but she sucked away at oranges and progressed from a liquid diet to the rice chop she loved.

"We made her a little dress and after the ward service on Sunday she trotted to the Children's Church, usually carrying the baby doll that she had acquired during her stay with us. She acted much older than her years—perhaps she had lost some of her babyhood as she had passed through this great ordeal—for she was only five. She would leave her bed in the ward and sit at the nurse's desk in the office just as if she were in charge of the whole show—as perhaps she was! She captured our hearts that first night and very soon had added to them the love and admiration of all the other patients, in fact all who knew her.

"Marie's wounds healed. We loved her so much it was difficult not to spoil her, to try to make up to her as far as we were able for all she had suffered. The time came when she was ready for discharge and she departed with her mother. I remember her so well that day—a brave little thing, hurrying off to the station to catch another train, walking beside her mother and carrying a miniature air bag we had found for her in which she had all her belongings. Many of us were a little tearful as we watched her go and our hearts were full of praise to God for His mercy and admiration of Marie for her wonderful will to live."

Lowell Gess tells that seven years later, when he was in Taiama, the girl and her mother surprised him when they came to see him. Marie was then a student in one of our mission schools.[10]

People now came from all over for eye and other surgery as well as for the medical clinics. Dr. Gess trained three young men to assist him in surgery. In 1960 there was a little girl, about two or three years old, who came in with a terrible tropical ulcer from her knee to the ankle on one leg. The mother consented to an amputation (which was unusual). She improved, though of course she had no leg.

In 1960, after nearly six months in "temporary" quarters, we were able to move back into a much enlarged and improved laboratory. It

Celebrating the new lab. Morlai Turay, Lab Assistant, offering squash to one of the nurses.

was a real joy to work in it, with lots of working space, cupboard space for storage, and even tile on the floor! We moved on a Wednesday afternoon after clinic, and on Friday I gave a "squash" party for the staff in celebration ("squash" to the English is not a vegetable but a drink!)

When I returned from furlough in 1959, after completing the work for a Master's Degree in Religious Education and being accepted for doctoral studies at Hartford Seminary Foundation in Hartford, Connecticut, I informed all those concerned that I would not be returning to Sierra Leone at the end of that term. Therefore, we began to look for a Sierra Leonean who had an educational background that would allow him to train as a certified medical technologist. Although Morlai had done faithful work he had only primary school education, and so did not qualify. The Conference found a teacher in Jaiama, and he was sent to Nigeria for the first part of his study. He then was to go to England for further study. Unfortunately, however, he died of typhoid while in Nigeria. Of the young men (in addition to Morlai) I had given elementary lab training, one died; one went to a government hospital, and only one went to the Jaiama Clinic. We had hoped to have one at Taiama, too. Some years later, when I returned to Sierra Leone as Area Secretary for West and North Africa, I visited Jaiama. The lab technician was still there, and he thanked me for what I had done. He said, "Miss Megill, you could have given me clothes, and they would have worn out; you could have given me other things, and they would not last; but you gave me the most important thing–an education."

I was sad when I heard after I left Sierra Leone that Morlai had died, also with an unknown viral disease. Although he and his wife were Christian, some of his family took him and gave him native medicine. While some of their medicines were helpful, others, especially if given in large doses or were the wrong kind, could be deadly. In Morlai's case his kidneys stopped functioning. They thought that someone had "wished" the sickness on him (witchcraft), and I think he may have believed it. He seemed to feel that the death of the young man who was to take my place was his fault, and that his illness was his punishment. Probably he was jealous of someone who would come and be over him, after the years he had worked faithfully at the hospital.

In 1961 my brother Don was with us for five months, along with his wife, Mary Alice. He was a medical student and had a Smith, Kline & French scholarship to work in a developing country. This counted as part of his training. Of course Dr. Silver gave her permission for him to come. Don and Mary Alice later returned as missionaries to Rotifunk for a three-year term (after I had left).

Don Megill, Medical Student

A visit to Shenge: Don, Mary Alice Megill,
Honoria Bailor, and a goat (a gift)

We had excitement of another kind in 1961 also, when two U.S. Navy helicopters landed on the school grounds near the hospital to bring us a big supply of medicine and drugs from the Christian Medical Society. There was a recording made for the Voice of America. (Good propaganda for the U.S.) Needless to say, there was a crowd of people who ran to see this strange and wonderful sight. We were very grateful for the medicines. That very day some of the vitamins were given to patients who came to the hospital, who could not afford to pay for such expensive medicines and yet needed them. We also had many tins (cans) of "Meals for Millions" which it was a pleasure to give to some of the undernourished people we saw every day, especially the children, some of whom were in such a terrible condition.

Chapter VII. Illness

<u>Ruth Harding</u>

It was not long after Gertrude and I arrived in Rotifunk that Ruth Harding became quite ill. She had two hospital experiences, but was with us in Rotifunk the rest of the time. This kept Dr. Silver going all the time, and for a long time she had no good night's sleep. She kept hoping that Ruth would get better, but no one was able to find out what was wrong with her, except that she was very susceptible to malaria and could tolerate few of the antimalarial drugs. But the doctor finally became convinced that the problem was a surgical one, as she became steadily worse. Ruth had been an inspiration to everyone who knew her. I had never seen anyone who had suffered so much and still kept a sunny disposition. She was, I believe, one of the best-loved missionaries ever to be in Africa. People were constantly asking about her. Finally the decision was made that she must get home, and as quickly as possible. So I went up to Jaiama where she was to be stationed, and collected her things. I went by train to Bo, a seven-hour trip. There the Leaders met me, and I stayed all night at their house. Then they drove me over to Jaiama–something which I appreciated very much, for no one knew I was coming, and it would have meant another train trip and then hiring a lorry to take me on to Jaiama. It is one hundred fifty miles from Bo to Jaiama, not a long distance in the States, but another matter in Africa. We left at 8:00 a.m. and arrived at Jaiama at 4:00 p.m. The Walkers were quite astonished to see us, but gave us good chop that night and beds to sleep in. We packed Ruth's things in two hours that night and the next day drove back to Bo. I stayed the night there, and then went to Rotifunk on Friday. Needless to say, I was quite tired when I got home, and also had a touch of fever. If it had not been such a sad occasion, I would have thoroughly enjoyed the trip. We drove through beautiful country which became quite hilly. It is higher and cooler there. We drove through rows of rubber trees part of the time, and at other times the ever-present "bush," with the inevitable palm trees. Frequently we passed places which had been brushed (that is, the bush and small trees cut down with a cutlass) and then burnt in preparation for making a farm. People were walking along the road with their bundles, some with loads of cassava stems on their head, taking them to the farms to plant. Much of the way was through Mende country, so I had a try at using a little of my Mende as we stopped at various places along the way. After leaving Mende country, we were in Kono country. The Konos have more round huts, in contrast to the square houses found in other parts of Sierra Leone. At Jaiama we had a boarding school, and were supposed to have a dispensary and small hospital, but there was no doctor or nurse there at that time. I didn't really see any of the mission, but the grounds around the medical residence were beautiful. There were orange, grapefruit, lime, and frangipanni trees, as well as many other kinds of trees and flowers.

Mrs. Leader came to Rotifunk on Monday to help us pack. I don't know what we would have done without her! The Freetown office was cabling everywhere trying to get plane reservations for Ruth and Dr. Silver–for Ruth was too ill to travel alone. On Wednesday they left Rotifunk by ambulance coach on a train. That was a sad day. Though we had tried to keep it from people until the last, to avoid a rush of visitors, there was a crowd gathered at the station and a procession followed as Ruth was carried down on a stretcher. There were many tearful goodbys. It was very hard on Ruth, for she never expected to come back to her beloved Africa again. (She did return eventually, but soon became ill again.)

It was an answer to prayer that they could get reservations so soon, and with few stopovers. From New York they flew to Cleveland, and then went on to the hospital where Ruth had taken her nurses' training.

Dr. Silver

It was April 16, 1953, in the third year of my first term in Sierra Leone. Gertrude Bloede had gone on furlough, and no one had been sent to replace her. I was concerned about Dr. Silver, for the load of work was too much for her, made doubly difficult because of the lack of a nurse. While we had African staff, who were very loyal, at that time the nurses had little training (more like nurses' aids). Ernest Kroma, our dispenser, was indispensable.

I knew that Dr. Silver had had a heart attack some years earlier. One evening at supper, I said to her, "Dr. Silver, I think you should tell me what I should do if you should have another heart attack."

She laughed, and said she would tell me if it came to that. I reminded her that she might not be able to tell me. So she told me what injection she should have.

It was only the next day that she came home very tired late in the afternoon, after seeing four hundred patients. I was in charge of housekeeping, and gave directions for meal preparation. When supper was ready, I went to her room where she was lying down, and called her. She said, "I think it is time for that injection." She was having severe pain from an angina attack. I ran to the hospital to see our head nurse, "Mama Abbie" (Abigail Johnson), and told her I needed her to bring the injection. I asked her not to tell anyone else what had happened. She gave the injection, and after a little while the doctor asked me to have the nurses bring over the charts for the patients in the hospital, as she wouldn't be able to go over! One did so, and she got up to write orders. A little later, a Lebanese woman came to the door, saying that a young woman patient we had seen that afternoon was coughing up blood. I had not had time to report the lab findings to the doctor, so I told her then that the sputum was full of tubercle bacilli. Since the Lebanese had more money, she told me to tell Mama Abbie to go give an injection of morphine to the patient, and then tell them to take her to Freetown (the capital city) as soon as possible.

I was very concerned, because I knew that Dr. Silver could have another attack and die at any time. So I went down the hill to the railroad station, and asked the Station Master if there was a goods (freight) coming through that night (I knew there were no passenger trains until the next day), as at that time there were no roads. I explained that I must get Dr. Silver to a doctor in Freetown, and asked if it would be possible for me to take her on the train. He was very willing to make arrangements, and I went back to see Ernest Kroma. I asked him not to tell anyone else because I knew a lot of people would be upset if they heard that Dr. Silver was so ill, but told him I would need him to come with some men at about 2:00 a.m. to carry her down on a lawn chair we had. I then went back and told the doctor of the arrangements I had made, and said, "You will go, won't you, Dr. Silver?" She gave an answer so typical of her--that she would, because if she didn't she knew it would be an extra worry for me!

It happened that an English woman, who was teaching at our Harford School for Girls, about twenty miles away, was with us in order to have a physical exam. I asked her to help me by packing a suitcase for Dr. Silver. When she finished, she said, "I have put in a pair of white gloves, too."

I said, "Why would she need white gloves?"

Her answer, "Well, you know that in Freetown she may need to go to some official event, where she would need the gloves!" It wasn't until later that I laughed about this. I am sure she had no idea how ill the doctor was.

I was able to get into a box car with the doctor as planned, and went on the trip of fifty-five miles--a very slow trip. I found that the Station Master had phoned the hospital in Freetown and talked to the head nurse (who was from Rotifunk, and had known Dr. Silver since she was a girl). At about 8:00 a.m. we reached the point where the road from Freetown ended, and she herself was there with an ambulance. I went with them to the hospital, and then went to the Mission House in the town. I had had no sleep all night, and of course had been under great stress. I was glad to eat a little breakfast, have a bath, and go to bed!

Later in the day I went to see Dr. Silver, and wrote down a list of instructions. I would not be able to treat any patients (legally), and would have to send them away. We had T.B. patients in the hospital which were being treated with a new medicine, and she told me the symptoms that might occur, in which case I should stop the medication. Some outpatients were taking a series of injections, and the dispenser and I could treat them.

I returned the next day to the hospital, where I was in charge! For the next two weeks I worked to close down the hospital. It was very difficult to send away people who had come from miles around, many of whom had no other place to go for medical treatment. To them, all white women in white uniforms were "doctors," and they could not understand why I could not treat them.

One evening a child was brought in with cerebral malaria (I confirmed that in the lab). I knew that if I sent her to Freetown she might not even reach there alive, let alone be able to see a doctor in time. So we admitted her, and I had the nurse give the injection of antimalarial medicine that Dr. Silver always ordered. That evening a nurse rushed to me at the house and said, "Miss Megill, that baby's dead." I went over to the hospital, where the mother was sitting on the floor with her dead child in her arms, weeping and moaning. I felt so bad, and thought, "If only I had been a doctor, perhaps I could have saved her."

The next day I wrote a rather angry letter to Dr. Heinmiller at the Board, accusing him of sending more doctors to Nigeria when we needed one so badly, and not supplying a replacement for Gertrude Bloede when she went on furlough. I had not realized that there was sensitivity after the recent (1946) church union between the former United Brethren Church (with a mission in Sierra Leone) and the Evangelical Church (their mission was in Nigeria). He had been Evangelical, so it seemed that I was accusing him of favoritism because of that. We had not paid much attention to that however, except to welcome some former Evangelicals as missionaries. He wrote back a letter that was not very consoling to me. (I guess he and Dr. Schaefer forgave me, since in later years they offered me the position on the Board of the new united church.)

Later, Dr. Silver recovered, and persuaded the doctor who took care of her to allow her to stay in Sierra Leone instead of returning to the States. Eventually, she came back to Rotifunk, supposedly to work part time. By then Ruth Harding had returned and Betty Beveridge, a midwife from England. Then both of them became ill with a mysterious viral disease which was never diagnosed–and that is another story!

Betty Beveridge

(The following is adapted from a paper written as an assignment for a course in writing at Hartford Seminary Foundation.)

It is always with a feeling of expectancy, of wondering, that one prepares to welcome a new missionary to her home and work. We had already heard of her "paper" qualifications–Sister Betty Beveridge, S.R.N., S.C.M., twenty years' experience as a nurse-midwife in London. (The title "Sister" meant that she was a senior nurse, not a Catholic or Episcopalian Sister. In fact, she was Baptist.) We had received a report from someone who had talked with her for a few hours. It sounded as if she was the answer to prayer so far as being someone who could share the heavy load of work at the hospital. But what was she like? What sort of person would we be living and working with intimately for the next years? How will she adapt to this situation? Will an English woman be able to live happily with Americans? Will she really identify herself with the people, and will they accept her? All these thoughts were in our minds as we prepared to meet her at the railroad station.

My first impressions were of a tall, well-built, athletic woman, with a friendly, self-confident air. She strode along the path, hands in pockets, occasionally, with a toss of her head and a quick thrust of fingers, pushing her hair impatiently out of her eyes. As the days passed, we saw that she was efficient, knew her work well, and would be willing to devote herself with tireless energy to the task. She seemed to be able to identify herself with others, and yet at times seemed most inconsiderate. She had a particularly tender spot in her heart for children, especially little boys. I thought I was beginning to know her.

And then something happened that gave an opportunity one seldom has to get to know a person. With terrifying suddenness, illness struck. For days Betty's life hung in balance. Dr. Silver, for whom we were worried because she herself was just recovering from her heart attack, was already working day and night to care for Ruth Harding, who was again seriously ill. Now in addition she has this responsibility. And always, there was the work at the hospital.

It was then that the mission superintendent sent word to Lois Olsen, the nurse-midwife at Taiama, that she was to go to Rotifunk. Reluctantly, she did as was asked, expecting to stay for only a short time. In the end she stayed for four months. She took over most of the medical work in the hospital. Also, in order to do what we could to give the doctor some rest, Lois and I took turns staying with the two ill women. Abbie Johnson, our faithful senior nurse, was also asked to help with nursing care of the two missionaries.

It was during these long nights of pain that I came really to know Betty. In her delirium, and under the influence of drugs, she opened, as it were, for brief intervals, windows into her life and thoughts. It was then that I learned that underneath that self-confident, efficient, fearless exterior, there was an underlying fear of inadequacy. She was particularly worried as to whether she, an English woman, would be accepted by a group of Americans. She was afraid that she would be sent home, a failure, because of her illness. And she must not fail, for she had come against the desires and with the protests of her friends and family. For the first time she had felt the security of being part of a Christian family, and now she was afraid she would have to leave. Although already one could see that at times she was domineering and had a strong sense of the importance of position and authority, now there was revealed a dependence upon and almost desperate need for the love of another. It was almost a possessive love, a mother-fixation, which she developed for the doctor.

Under the confident exterior there was also revealed the fear with which she had lived during the war, as she went through the streets of London to a delivery case, bombs falling all around her; as she reassured the patients and helped them to crawl under their beds when an alarm sounded. Now, all the terrible fear was revealed as the rumble of the thunder of an approaching tropical storm was transformed by her delirium into the roar of planes carrying their rain of death.

Her love of poetry and sensitivity for the beautiful were revealed as she quoted verse after verse of Scripture, Shakespeare, Wordsworth; her constant involvement in her work as she rehearsed delivery after delivery in her delirium. So it was, in this experience, that I began to understand what sort of person Betty really was. It was almost as if I had entered a sacred place unbidden.

All efforts to make a diagnosis of the illness of the two patients came to naught. Dr. Silver consulted with African and expatriate doctors. She even had me draw blood, which we sent to the hospital at the University of Ibadan in Nigeria, but they found nothing. Both the patients were adamant against being sent home, and Dr. Silver kept hoping that they would improve. She asked us not to let the Board executive in Dayton know of the situation. Therefore we did not, but each day Lois and I wondered how long the situation could continue.

Finally, after Ruth had been ill for four months, a British Methodist nurse returning to England offered to take her along. As the ship traveled north, her condition improved. There were numerous tests in London, but the cause of her illness was never found. She returned to the States, where she eventually recovered.

I had delayed my furlough, so I eventually left for the States. Since Betty was making no improvement, Dr. Silver finally decided to take her to Britain. In the meantime word came that Dr. Silver had been awarded the honor of Member of the British Empire (M.B.E.) by the Queen, part of the 1953 birthday honors list. It was the first time an American citizen had been so honored in Sierra Leone. This was to have been presented to her on New Year's Day in a formal ceremony by the Governor General. Due to the emergency the medal was given to her in a private ceremony.

Lois went to Freetown and to the airport to see them off. Betty was carried on a stretcher and was heavily sedated. Lois describes it thus: "This was before the days of jet aircraft, and the trip from Lagos, Nigeria to London took three days. The passengers spent the nights in a hotel on the ground, and the plane even landed at noon for lunch."[11]

Betty eventually recovered, though again, the disease was never diagnosed. She later returned to Sierra Leone, where she became ill again. However, she eventually recovered completely.

The Lady With The Healing Hand

DEN SAY [pen name of the writer]--Florence Nightingale has been immortalized as The Lady with the Lamp. Readers of history are familiar with the records of the Crimean War. Men are always grateful to life savers, doctors and nurses are in the enviable position of being life-savers.

Dr. Mabel Silver has placed Rotifunk Hospital on the Map. Her name has been a household word not only in the Protectorate, but in the Colony. Years ago Conakry [French Guinea] was the regular resort of many of our people who sought recovery from the hand of a French Doctor there when local remedy failed.

Rotifunk was the Protectorate (bush) counterpart for those who could not afford the Conakry trip; so many were the callers at Rotifunk that restrictions had to be placed on those who disregarded their own local medical facilities and sought admission for treatment there. How often have many not declared their domicile for some portion of the Protectorate only to secure treatment! Dr. Silver has been awarded "Honour" by the Queen. Her patients who have received treatment from her many who owe their lives and health to her painstaking treatment--and they number by the thousands--hail her today as their Doctor Queen. We joy in this recognition of the services of "The Lady with the Healing Hand."

[From a Freetown newspaper--probably the *Daily Mail*.]

Chapter VIII. More Christian Education

<u>Women's Work: the trip to Mogbainchain</u>

Before and after the events described in the previous chapter I became more and more involved in various aspects of Christian education. After our successful Women's Institute in 1951 Honoria and I decided to try an even more ambitious one the next year, and invite women from other parts of Sierra Leone. We decided, first, to contact the women of two other churches in the district to see if they would be willing to help share the expense and the responsibility of being hostesses with the Rotifunk women. So Honoria and I and two other women made a trip on the goods (freight) train one Saturday morning to Bradford, a village not far from Rotifunk, and talked to the women there. They agreed to help us and to send representatives to Rotifunk to help plan. Then, the next weekend, we went on a longer and most interesting trip. This time the trip was by launch down the river to the small Sherbro village of Mogbainchain. A number of us went–the same who went to the other town, and Dr. Smith and several older boys and children. We were supposed to start on the launch with the tide at 2:30 p.m., but the launch failed to show up until 8:00. Then we had confusion about oil and gasoline, and by the time we got started it was nearly 9:00. We arrived near the village of Mogbainchain at about 10:30–then our trouble started. The Bumpe River is a tidal river and because we had been so delayed, we were left stranded in deep mud in the small branch of the river. So two of the older boys had to wade hip-deep through the mud for a quarter of a mile to reach land, and then walk a mile to the village. The people had waited for us until just before the time we arrived, but finally went home. At about 12:00 a whole group of men and boys from the village arrived. They carried loads and some of the children out on their shoulders and through the mud. Then they pushed a long canoe through the mud to the launch, and the rest of us got in. And how they did work to push the canoe inches at a time through that sticky mud! Finally, after carrying more people out, and pushing with all their might, we arrived on dry land. Then there was a mile walk through the bush path with only the light of a lantern. By the time we tumbled into bed at 2:00 a.m., we were too tired to bother about mosquito nets (it really didn't make much difference since we had been out all night anyway.)

The next morning we met with a group of the leaders of the church and greeted them in the native fashion. That meant having Dr. Smith give greetings and passing one pound note to me; then I passed it to another person, she to another, and finally to Honoria Bailor. Everyone said some word of greeting and appreciation as they passed the money on. Then Mrs. Bailor handed the money to one of their people, and it was passed from one person to another, each making appropriate comments and thanking us until it reached the "big" man. That afternoon, they all gathered to greet us the same way and gave us rice and a goat to take home with us.

During the church service I spoke and Mrs. Bailor interpreted; Dr. Smith and she sang and helped in other ways. (Honoria told me afterward that the reason she laughed in the middle of interpreting some of my most earnest statements was that someone spoke out loud, saying, "Oh, look! She has open teeth!")

The Mogbainchain church is a wonderful example of a really indigenous church. In 1947 there was a mild earthquake in Sierra Leone. Some of the people of this village were so frightened and awed that they started to pray, lead by a student from a mission school. After that they decided that a God so wonderful was one they wanted to worship, and so they started gathering for prayers

and church services on the veranda of one of the houses. After a few months they started building a church for themselves. The men dug the dirt and cut sticks; the women carried water and daubed mud; and the children helped, too. For quite a long time they worshiped in this small church, but they outgrew it, and so at the time we were there were just completing a larger church. All this was done with no help from the mission. They met every morning and every evening for prayers (since the Muslims did so, they felt they should too.) That year they were making a church farm. There was no pastor or village worker; they were all nonliterate, except for one young man who had finished Standard VI (grade 8). He led the church services for them and taught them hymns. Occasionally, teachers and other workers from Rotifunk went to hold services for them. It was really a thrill to talk with such a group of Christians.

After the church service we talked with the women about plans for a meeting and invited the men to stay, since they would have to give permission for their wives to attend the meeting in Rotifunk. They agreed to help with whatever we asked for and to attend.

After eating plenty of rice and pineapple, we left in the afternoon for Rotifunk and arrived home by dark.

After much planning and hard work, we started our Women's Institute on Friday, May 16, and continued until Monday. We met the women who came on the train, took them to the places they were to stay, and then fed them all rice in one of the hospital buildings. Six women came from Mogbainchain, walking overland ten miles. Four of them arrived before the others, carrying two bushels of rice and a bottle of palm oil, plus their own belongings, and a baby. Can you imagine women in America doing that?

We had twenty-nine women from different places, and many attended from Rotifunk. Our average attendance was about sixty, except that at our Sunday night meeting we had one hundred three, for we invited the men and boys then. We met each morning except Sunday for morning devotions; then the women were served tea and met again at 10:00. We had Bible study, conducted by Vivian Olson, discussion of Women's Work by Cora Horst, devotional talks by her and others, a health talk by Dr. Silver, demonstration of soap making, and singing. Everything had to be interpreted from English to Krio, Temne, and Mende. You can imagine what a problem that made. We sang hymns in Mende, Temne and Sherbro, as well as Krio "shouts," as they are called. On Sunday during Sunday

School hour those who wished attended the vernacular services–we held Mende, Temne and Sherbro services in different places. On Sunday afternoon about sixty women walked through Rotifunk and on to a small village about a mile and a half away. It made a long, colorful procession, with everyone dressed in bright Creole "prints" or bubas and lappas. We sang as we went and then held a service in Temne for the people there when we reached the village.

On Saturday morning, Cora Horst was in charge of a session when we shared experiences in women's work. The Mogbainchain women told how they had helped build the church and said that since they were all nonliterate they didn't understand very much, but they were trying to worship God as they knew Him. They asked that we pray for them and help them in any way we could. Other women told of victories and needs in their groups, and they, too, asked for prayers.

On Sunday night we used an adaptation of one of the meetings sent out for new W.S.W.S. societies, with the theme of women and their homes. Through pantomime and song we showed the influence of Christian women. This was the thing we needed to emphasize; for most women at that time spent almost all of their time in the home and had no responsibility in the church. So we tried to lead them to think of the importance of raising children in a Christian way and helped them to see that their work in the home could be consecrated to the Lord. At the close of the meeting I asked any who wished to bring their offering to the altar and give some word of testimony, praise, thanksgiving, Bible verse, or song. There was a steady stream of women to the altar. Then we continued singing, in various languages, until after about forty-five minutes we closed the meeting.

On Monday we who had been responsible for the meeting all gave a sigh of relief when the last group was seen off on the train; but I am sure that most of us, at least, had very pleasant memories of the real Christian fellowship that we had had–even though we represented two nations, about five different tribes, literate and nonliterate, and could not even talk directly to one another in many cases because of the language differences. But the Spirit of God was there!

From that time on, Institutes were held regularly, and also Annual Meetings, after a W.S.W.S. (Women's Society of World Service) was organized.

Ruth Gess, giving health talk
Musu Morsay, interpreter
Women's Institute 1959

W.S.W.S. Convention, Bo, 1960
Women Eating

Conference Children's Director; Youth Camps

By 1957 I had been appointed Conference Children's Director, so that made me a member of the Board of Christian Education, which meant more work. I then discovered that "Children's Work" also included youth camps! The first youth camp had been held in 1955. I helped them to divide the camp into two, for two different age groups. Missionaries and Africans (usually teachers) were leaders in the camps. It was good that Christian young people could meet together for work, play, study and worship. A number of young people made decisions for Christ, or rededications, or pledged themselves to enter some kind of Christian service. During the years following Sierra Leoneans took over more and more of the leadership.

Junior Youth Camp, Moyamba, 1960
Natalie Closson with Craft Group

Doris Caulker Leads Games

Adventure Group–Max and Ada Bailor

Christian Family Week

Another venture was a Christian Family Week, which we held at Rotifunk for the first time in October of 1957. We began the week with a service on Sunday evening. On Wednesday there was an exhibit of Home Arts and Crafts where women exhibited handwork and various articles of food they had made. There were judges, and on Friday night during the Fellowship Night prizes were given. Some of the nonliterate women won prizes as well as those who had had opportunities for education. That night there were games and singing and then refreshments of tea and sandwiches. The church was packed. Each night we stressed families attending in groups, and the family which attended each night was presented with a picture for their home. One of the workmen at the hospital received the prize. We hoped that the week's observance helped people realize a little better just what a Christian home should be. There was great need for more Christian homes, for there were so few. The Christian Family Week was climaxed by the annual Woman's Day observance. The women had charge of an early morning vernacular service and the regular morning worship service in English, and presented a play in the evening.

Kindergarten Church School

By 1957 I had begun another new venture in the church at Rotifunk, by starting, in addition to the Nursery Church School, which was going well, a Kindergarten class for five-year-olds who had just started to school. I wrote a one-year course on "Discoveries in God's World" for that age group, and, as I did for the nursery materials, tried it at Rotifunk before introducing it to other churches. We held leadership training camps to introduce the new program and materials to other churches.

Leadership Training, Rotifunk–Telling Stories

Sunday was very busy for me. With our school of nearly six hundred we were actually reaching only a small percentage through the church. And yet, we had so many children that I hardly knew what to do with them with the limited facilities and the number of trained leaders that we had. For example, on one Sunday we had twenty-three children in the nursery; twenty-three in kindergarten; and one hundred fifteen in the primary division of the Children's Church, which we had for children from Class II to Standard III. We prepared outdoor shelters for the two younger groups, and the older children met at the school. I had hoped to eventually have separate age groups for all the children, but it was not possible to develop the materials and train the teachers before I left Sierra Leone. (I was surprised to learn several years later when one of the Sierra Leone students at Trinity Theological College in Ghana, where I was then teaching, told me he had been in my children's church. He became a teacher, and was holding Children's Church at Rotifunk using some of the materials I had adapted years before for use there.)

Kindergarten Church School

Carrying the Baby on her Back

Bathing the Baby

Water Play–Boats

Collecting Tadpoles

Spatter Painting

Rhythmic Games

Jungle Gym

Slide

Esther L. Megill

Christian Education Curriculum for the Schools

The church also asked us to develop Christian education materials to use in their primary schools. We formed a committee, and several of us worked long hours writing the materials. My sister-in-law, Mary Alice Megill, who was at Rotifunk at that time with Don when he was working with Dr. Silver, did much of the typing. That helped a great deal. We eventually prepared materials for each class, including some music on records to be used with it. What we lacked were pictures, but we had no way to obtain these. We held courses to train teachers to use the material in the schools.

Training for teachers in the schools–New Religious Education Curriculum

A Children's Prayer Book

During my last year in Sierra Leone I produced a children's prayer book, called *Father, We Thank Thee.* I asked two friends to translate the English words, one into Temne and one into Mende, so that the little book had the prayer in three languages. I illustrated it with photographs I had taken and developed in our bathroom. (The night watchman would ask me, "Miss Megill, are you going to wash pictures tonight?" If I said yes, he would begin pumping water from the cistern into the tank in the attic, so that I could have a steady supply of water. The photography work had to be done at night in order to have a perfectly dark room. It would also be very hot, with the door and the window closed!) The book was published in 1962 by The Provincial Literature Bureau in Bo, and printed in England. In 1967 the United Society for Christian Literature in Zambia published it in three languages, Nyanja, Bemba, and Shona.

I was able to do much of the Christian education work during times when there was no doctor at Rotifunk, so that I was not kept so busy in the laboratory.

Children of Sierra Leone

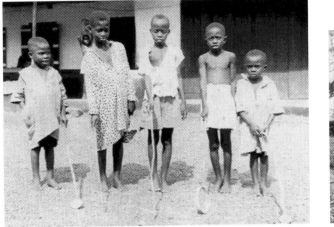

Boys with toys they have made

Morning Prayers

A Ware* Game

85

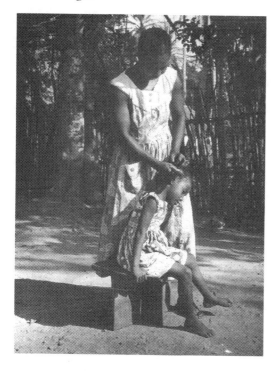

Braiding Hair

Mother Cooking

Going on an errand for Mother

At the Baby Clinic

Baby's First Steps

Caring for Baby

"Brooking" (Washing) Clothes

Sweeping the Yard

Serving the "stranger" (guest)

Helping Mother bathe the baby

Morning Tea

Bananas

Playing at Waterside

Bird's Nest

Dog with Puppies

Playing "Cook"

Chapter IX. Centenary Celebration–One Hundred Years in Sierra Leone!

"Christian missions are as old as the day our Lord commissioned His disciples to 'Go forth and teach all nations.' From that day to the present Christian missionaries have gone all over the world . . . It is now one hundred years since [United Brethren mission work] began in our own land of Sierra Leone . . . Forward with Christ!"–Solomon B. Caulker, from the pageant he wrote to celebrate the 100th anniversary of the work of the U.B./E.U.B. mission in Sierra Leone.

Sierra Leone was the first overseas country to which the United Brethren in Christ Church sent missionaries. W. J. Shuey, D. K. Flickinger, and Daniel Kumler arrived in 1855. They did not settle in Freetown, in the Colony, but went instead down the coast and eventually decided to settle in Shenge. There were some years of struggle as missionaries rapidly came and went–many of them becoming ill or dying in this area that was called "The White Man's Graveyard." After several years there were two converts. One of them was Lucy Caulker, age fourteen, the daughter of the chief, and grandmother of Honoria Bailor. Discouraging years followed, and at one time the Board was nearly ready to give up on their mission in Africa. Then Joseph Gomer and his wife answered the call, and did, it was reported, "phenomenal work." In 1877 the Women's Missionary Association sent their first missionary, Miss Emily Beeken, to Rotifunk. She was followed later by others, including those who were killed in the 1898 massacre.

A. C. Spangler, Mrs. Mary Hough,
Bishop Warner

During the 75th Annual Conference the Centenary celebration began, and continued through the year. A deputation from the Department of World Mission was welcomed, Bishop I. D. Warner, Mrs. S. S. Hough, and Mr. A. C. Spangler. The first welcome was in our Mission Council session the evening of January 4, and then the public church welcome was in King Memorial Church on January 6, 1955. A general welcome service was also given by the United Christian Council, at which time they were greeted by the Mayor of Freetown and heads of the chief churches in Freetown.

The Conference began January 8 and continued with business sessions and committee meetings. On Saturday afternoon there was a big tea party in Victoria Park, where a large crowd of people met. The Governor was represented by the Acting Colonial Secretary. The Police Band provided enjoyable music.

Sunday was always the big day of our Conference, and as Miss Vesper reported, that day was no exception, for King Memorial Church, the large E.U.B. church in Freetown, was filled long before the ringing of the last bell. Bishop Ira D. Warner preached the sermon, reviewing the work of the past one hundred years and challenged those present to greater service in the coming years. The women of King Memorial Church served a delicious dinner to all who wanted to remain.

Dr. Silver greets Bishop Warner

In the afternoon members of the church, pastors, teachers, Boy Scouts, Girl Guides and friends, led by the West African Frontier Force Band, paraded from Albert Academy, our large boys' school, to the Elizabeth II playing field, where a great service of Thanksgiving was held. The Bishop again preached to a large crowd, and a choir gave several selections.

On Monday afternoon the women representatives from the different churches in Freetown and the Protectorate met in business session, and then in the evening had Women's Night, always one of the high points of the Conference. We were privileged to have as the speaker Mrs. S. S. Hough.[12] She and her husband, Rev. I. E. Albert, came to Africa in 1899 to rebuild and reestablish the church and school at Shenge after the uprising in 1898. In 1902 her husband died by drowning in the Bumpe River near Rotifunk (possibly he had a heart attack first), and is buried there. Mrs. Albert and her little daughter stayed until 1903. She had not been back to Sierra Leone since, so this was a great event for her.

Tuesday night a pageant, "Forward with Christ," written and directed by the Rev. S. B. Caulker,[13] was given at Albert Academy to a large and appreciative audience. The pageant dramatized the history of the U.B./E.U.B. church in Sierra Leone. It ended with the roll call of The Evangelical United Brethren Church, as representatives came forward from the different tribes, singing their hymns in their own languages–Sherbro, Mende Temne, Kono and Kissi. Then came others, including the teachers, school children, doctors and nurses, as well as those representing Women's Work. All came singing and continued to sing as they stood around the cross. This ended the beautiful and effective pageant which left a lasting impression upon all who saw it.

After the Conference the deputation from the United States started a tour of the churches of the Conference, beginning at Rotifunk. On Saturday morning two of the deputation accompanied by some of us missionaries stationed at Rotifunk and several African pastors traveled by launch to Mogbainchain to visit the youngest church of the Conference, and returned to Rotifunk that night. On Sunday morning the group divided into two preaching teams. One team went to Bradford (a nearby town), and the other remained at Rotifunk. Before the service that morning we formed a procession to the missionary cemetery, where a short service was held, with the Bishop, Rev. T. B. Williams and Rev. W. B. Claye (present pastor at Rotifunk) in charge. A short address was given by Mr. Moses Barley. Wreaths made from the flowers of the frangipani tree growing in the cemetery were presented by Miss Christiana Caulker to Mrs. Hough to be laid on the graves of her husband and other missionaries buried there. We solemnly walked out of the cemetery after the benediction to the processional hymn, "Onward Christian Soldiers" and went to the church for the service there. Mrs. Hough was the guest speaker, and surveyed the missionary endeavors since 1890 to the present time. Her challenge to us was "Pray for a revival for this church." The service was followed by a banquet in honor of the deputation, held in the church yard. More than three hundred members of the church attended. The events of the Sunday ended with a service in which the Bishop showed slides and preached. More than four hundred attended this closing service.[14]

Chapter X. Harford School
"My year of part-time teaching at Harford is one of fond memories."

In February of 1957 I began a new venture, one that proved to be most rewarding. Our Harford School for Girls was at Moyamba, just eighteen miles from us, but at that time easily available only by rail. A new road was nearly complete, but we had no vehicle at Rotifunk. At that time the school had a critical shortage of teachers. In fact, from year to year they wondered how they were even going to open school. It was only because missionary teachers were doing impossible jobs that it did stay open. Because I had previously taught science in high school, and there was no doctor at the time at Rotifunk, they asked whether I could teach biology to Form V, the top class. There were seven girls in the class, who were preparing to take the all-important Cambridge Examination which meant so much under the English educational system. I found that I really enjoyed teaching again, for the girls were so eager to learn. I went to Moyamba on the "Express" train each Friday morning (it took one and a half hours to go the eighteen miles). If it was on time (which it wasn't, usually) I got there in time to set up some experiments and get ready for class. Fortunately, I could do some preparation in the lab at the hospital during the week. One week, for example, the train, which was due at 10:00 a.m., arrived at 11:00. We had to stop once on the way to get up enough steam to get up a hill, and once when apparently the engine driver and someone else were having a fight! I got into my classroom at 1:30. The class was supposed to begin at 1:00, but I could keep the girls overtime in the afternoon if I wished, since they had no other classes. The people from Harford then drove me back to Rotifunk each Friday evening.

When it was time for the next term of school Wavelene Babbitt, who was principal at the time, asked whether I could come on Thursday and teach Form IV biology also, in the morning. Because of the shortage of teachers they were wondering whether they would have to cut the number of classes or girls, though they had just finished a building program which included a new dormitory, dining room, and staff houses.

By December I was going to Moyamba each Wednesday, and teaching seven periods a day for two days. In this way I was able to take care of all four biology classes. Then I added a General Science class on Wednesday evenings! I enjoyed my teaching very much. I wrote in a letter at that time, "In times of discouragement over some difficulties at Rotifunk, it has been my contact with the girls there, as I see some of them planning for lives of service in the near future and hear their Christian testimonies, that gives me hope for the church in Sierra Leone."

At that time, in addition to taking examinations set by England, we also used British text books. This meant, for example, that the flower which was discussed in the text book was the buttercup, which did not grow in Sierra Leone. Yet we had a variety of flowers all year around. I decided, therefore, that I would get samples of the flowers they knew for study. They learned the parts of the flower, made drawings, learned how they were pollinated. Then on the first examination I gave them, I asked them to draw a flower, label the parts, and tell how it was pollinated. And everyone drew the buttercup! I asked them why–and they said, "It was easier, because it was in the book." So, the next time, I said, "Draw a flower <u>you have seen</u> . . . "

At another time I had the girls collect cashews from the tree. This was not in the form of the nuts we know. The "Cashew fruit" is actually a swollen peduncle, large and pulpy, that grows behind the real fruit which yields the cashew nut. The cashew nut grows externally in its own kidney shaped hard shell at the end of this pseudo-fruit or peduncle. The juice is quite corrosive, though I did not know it at the time. The girls drew the parts for their lab work. The next week when I returned, June Hartranft told me that they had used the juice to write initials of their favorite friends on their thighs. This had caused blisters, and the initials were there permanently. It also gave them a fever, and some were really ill. She told me that the day previously she had insisted that they march for the Empire Day celebration, in their stiffly starched dresses. I said to them, "You knew what would happen, though I didn't. Why did you do it?" That is a question, of course, that one might as well not ask a teen-ager!.

There was little lab equipment–one microscope, as I recall. We were not able to send away for specimens as was done in the United States. So, I began to gather specimens wherever I could. Instead of frogs (which are hard to catch), we dissected toads. When we needed cockroaches, I asked our cook at Rotifunk if he could get me some. He said, "Oh, yes, Miss Megill–just give me a yar [Temnes had difficulty pronouncing "j"] with some "yam" and I will take it to my house. I will get you plenty of cockroaches there." And he did–big ones, too!

I really hated the educational method that almost forced us to teach for exams. When I saw that the syllabus did not contain mosses or reptiles, I decided that I would <u>not</u> teach biology in Africa without dealing with these–so I put them into my syllabus. Because the girls were allowed to study previous exams, they began to suspect that I was teaching them some things that were not in the syllabus, so they asked me. I said, "Yes, I am, because I am teaching you biology, not just to pass an exam." They wanted me to tell them what I was adding, because they would then know what to study the hardest. Of course, I would not do that. And, when they returned from taking the exam I discovered that they had included both mosses and reptiles!

At one time we took them to the government agricultural station at Njala for a field trip. There we saw hens which were producing eggs–I pointed out that there were no roosters with the hens. The girls had insisted that hens could not lay eggs unless there was a rooster. There was also a belief that the small eggs that young pullets lay were laid by the roosters. I reminded them that if they looked at the anatomy, there was no way a rooster could lay eggs!

Form V Girls in Biology Lab
Miattu Kroma and Mary Cobinah

In the Library

Relaxing in the Dormitory

Form V Classroom

Domestic Science Girls–Sally Kamara,
Gladys Williams

June Hartranft, Principal, 1958

Marching to Church

Chapel

In December of that year we had an open house at Harford, and I was responsible to help Form III set up a science exhibit. They were very enthusiastic about it, and named practically all the experiments we had done when we made a list of what to show. On Saturday night was the school closing program; Sunday there were special services. The next day the two school-leaving classes, Form IV, Domestic Science, and Form V, School Certificate, left. The Form V girls had almost two weeks of school certificate examinations before them. I was very pleased when they all did well. By the next term they were able to find more teachers, so I did not teach again at Harford. However, I felt that many of the girls were my friends. A few of them came to Rotifunk for training as midwives. As the years passed, many of the leaders not only in the church but also in government were graduates of Harford School. When I returned for some volunteer work in 1989 there were several times that women who had been my students recognized me on the street or elsewhere, and came enthusiastically to greet me.

After independence Sierra Leone developed its own text books, and a West African School Certificate examination was set up to take the place of the British Cambridge Examination.

A new experiment was tried that year when the Form V boys from Albert Academy, our secondary school for boys in Freetown, came to visit the Form V girls at Harford. There were eleven boys and seven girls. The girls fed them a good meal of Jollof rice, and beat the boys overwhelmingly in a game of volley ball! We were glad for Christian young people to have a chance to know one another in a wholesome way. Many of these young people had spent most of their lives in a boarding home where they had little chance to learn to know members of the opposite sex; and it was against the custom of the older generation for young people to mix in such informal ways. We felt it was important for them to do so, if they were to fit themselves into modern society, and learn to live according to Christian standards.

In November of 1960 the "old girls" (alumnae) of Harford School celebrated the 60th Anniversary of the founding of the school. Hundreds of them returned to Harford for a five-day celebration. Many dignitaries were there, including Paramount Chief Madam Ella Koblo-Gulama, chief at Moyamba, who was also a graduate of Harford. Miss Mary McLanachan, editor of *The World Evangel*, was with us for our annual W.S.W.S. Convention, and for the Harford celebration. She wrote in an editorial in the *Evangel* about this event:[15]

The days in Moyamba at the Harford School for Girls are certainly ones which *I will remember.* What a sight to see the 239 students in their school uniforms marching to chapel, to church, in the anniversary parades! And what a challenge it was to speak to them as it was my privilege to do four times. Other high points–visiting classes and chatting with the girls on campus; fellowship with African and missionary staff members; Thanksgiving dinner with African and missionary friends; the hospitality of the missionaries; the beautiful campus itself.

The 60th Anniversary Celebration of Harford School was indeed a high point . . . [It] was planned and carried out by the Old Girls (Alumni) . . . Beginning with the Reunion Service Friday afternoon, November 25, which opened the celebration; the Service of Reminiscences that evening and the torch light parade through the town afterward; the delightful tea party on Saturday afternoon, presided over so graciously by Madam Gulama, when a huge anniversary cake with 60 candles was cut by the Old Girl from the first class and the youngest present student (eleven years old); the Sunday morning service of worship and communion in the church and the Thanksgiving service in the afternoon; culminating with the picnic Monday afternoon–these days and these experiences *I will remember* always.

Natalie Closson, Winifred Bradford, Mary McLanachan,
and attendees at the W.S.W.S. Convention Bo, 1960
Lunch time

She also spent Christmas with us at Rotifunk. She told us that once at breakfast, June Hartranft, the principal, said, "Oh, my, we have forgotten our prayers this morning!" Miss McLanachan said that they had had prayer so many times during the day that if they had prayed again the Lord would have said, "What, Harford School again?" I was sorry that I was unable to attend that celebration, but my year of part-time teaching at Harford is one of fond memories.

Chapter XI. Independence!

In May of 1960 a group of the country's leaders returned from constitutional talks in London. The whole country was jubilant over the promise of independence in April 1961. Everywhere we heard the word "Independence!" Some realized, however, that there was much work to be done before that time and that if there was really to be freedom, there must be hard work, an increased sense of responsibility, and a unity which was often lacking in the country. Some of the men trained in the E.U.B. Church schools had important responsibilities during those times, as, for example our Premier Sir Milton Margai and Dr. John Karefa-Smart, one of the ministers of government. But everywhere we heard the word, "Independence!" The newspaper came out each day with "____ Days Until Independence" in a prominent place on the front pages. We frequently heard from the nearby school the words of the new national anthem which the children were practicing. The words were written by C. Nelson Fyle, a native of Freetown and the music by John Akar, a native of Rotifunk, chosen from those submitted for a national competition.

The words are:

High we exalt thee, realm of the free.

Great is the love we have for thee;

Firmly united, ever we stand

Singing thy praise, O native land.

We raise up our hearts and voices on high;

The hills and the valleys re-echo our cry.

Blessing and peace be ever thine own,

Land that we love, our Sierra Leone.

One with a faith that wisdom inspires,

One with a zeal that never tires,

Ever we seek to honour thy name,

Ours is the labour, thine the fame.

We pray that no harm on thy children may fall,

That blessing and peace may descend on us all;

So may we serve thee ever alone

Land that we love, our Sierra Leone.

Knowledge and truth our forefathers spread,

Mighty the nations whom they led.

Mighty they made thee, so too may we

Show forth the good that is ever in thee.

We pledge our devotion, our strength and our might

Thy cause to defend and to stand for thy right.

All that we have is ever thine own;

Land that we love, our Sierra Leone.

Designs were also submitted for a flag. The one finally selected had three horizontal stripes of equal width, green at the top, white in the middle and blue below. Green stood for Sierra Leone's agriculture and the natural resources in her mountains; White, for unity and justice; and Blue, for the hope that Sierra Leone's unique harbor might make its contribution to peace throughout the world in the years ahead.[16]

The great day came on April 27, 1961. On the evening of the 26th several of us drove over to Moyamba for the ceremonies which marked the birth of a new nation. We went to the field at 10:00 p.m. and watched traditional dancing, a "march past" of school children, Boy Scouts, Boys' Brigade, and the forming of the Guard of Honour. As it neared midnight, we stood and sang the British national anthem. Then just at midnight the Union Jack was lowered and the new Sierra Leone flag was raised. It was an impressive moment. There were cheers as the flag was raised, and then we all joined in singing the Sierra Leone national anthem. There were several speeches, a fireworks display and more dancing afterward, but we left before everything was finished, since we still had an hour's drive back to Rotifunk.

> "We are a free nation, but there is much to be done that lies ahead of us . . . We should work very hard if we are to achieve success, for what is freedom if we do not work to achieve it culturally, scientifically, technically, economically and spiritually?"
>
> –Zainabu Kamara

Independence Celebration at Rotifunk
April 27, 1961

Then next day, Thursday, we watched traditional dancing there, and then on Friday, also a holiday, several of us went to Shenge for a day at the beach. (It took me some time to recover from a severe sunburn and a "jigger"* in my foot–all the price for a wonderful day!)

We were thankful that, unlike in some other countries, there was little disturbance during the changeover in government. There were some troublemakers in Freetown, but a number of the ring-leaders were arrested before Independence; and so there was no trouble during the celebrations there. In Freetown, of course, there were several days of ceremonies and celebrations of various sorts. The Duke of Kent was there as a personal representative of the Queen, and presented the Constitutional Instruments to the Prime Minister, Sir Milton Margai, in an impressive ceremony on the 27th.

In an article in the October 1961 *World Evangel*, Zainabu Kamara, a graduate and later a teacher at Harford School, wrote that when friends asked how they got on with the British, "their masters," she answered, "Though we are not an independent people, yet we are not oppressed at all by the British; but neither have we fully enjoyed what we rightfully feel is ours. However, in comparison with our sister countries like Algeria, the Congo, and South Africa, we are in Paradise." Then she continued, "We are a free nation, but there is much to be done that lies ahead of us . . . We should work very hard if we are to achieve success, for what is freedom if we do not work to achieve it culturally, scientifically, technically, economically and spiritually?"

However, in the years since, unfortunately, there were corrupt leaders, continued poverty and hardship for many people. More will be written later about the disastrous civil war which lasted for twelve years.

Sierra Leone was admitted to the United Nations on September 27, 1961 as the one hundredth member.

Chapter XII. The Installation of a Chief

"He that ruleth over men must be just, ruling in the fear of God." 2 Samuel 23:3

For some years our good friend Honoria Bailor had wanted to become Paramount Chief of the Kargboro Chiefdom, with Shenge as the chief's residence. In the Sherbro tribe women could become a chief, though that was not true in some others. One stood for election, but must show that he or she was a legitimate descendent of a chief. Honoria's grandmother, Lucy Caulker, was the daughter of a chief, and thus she was eligible to stand for the chieftaincy herself. The first time she tried, she did not succeed. But on December 16, 1961, she was elected Paramount Chief of the Kargboro Chiefdom, and took the name of P.C. Madam Honoria Bailor-Caulker.

On Sunday, May 6, 1962, hundreds of people traveled the roads to Shenge to attend the formal installation and dedication service of Madam Honoria Bailor-Caulker as Paramount Chief of the Kargboro Chiefdom. Many E.U.B. missionaries, paramount chiefs, ambassadors, and other government officials, as well as members of the Caulker family and many of her subjects were present to give honor to the new Chief.

Since the roof of the Shenge Gomer Memorial Church had been removed in preparation for renovation, a roof of palm branches, bamboo, and sticks decorated with brilliantly colored tropical leaves made a pleasant shade within the church building. Only a small part of the crowd was able to sit in the church, while others sat on benches outside under palm shelters. Close by was the grave of her grandmother, Lucy B. Caulker, one of the first converts to Christianity.

The service began with a procession of the Chief, followed by her tribal authorities and family members, with a guard of honor of the local Boy Scouts and Girl Guides and court messengers. The music was furnished by the Sierra Leone Police Band. Rev. J. K. Fergusson of Moyamba conducted the service. Rev. B.A. Carew, superintendent of the Bo District; Rev. W. G. T. M. Wolseley of Kenema, a cousin of the chief; Rev. E. G. Taylor, the local pastor; Rev. Clyde Galow, Field Representative of the Division of World Missions, Evangelical United Brethren Board of Missions; and Dr. C. W. Leader all took part in the impressive service of worship. Dr. S. M. Renner, superintendent of the Freetown District, preached the sermon, using as his texts Daniel 11:32b,

" . . .The people that do know their God shall be strong, and do exploits," and 2 Samuel 23:3, "He that ruleth over men must be just, ruling in the fear of God." In his stirring message, Dr. Renner challenged the Chief to rule her people in justice, tempered with mercy. He spoke of the challenge and opportunities a ruler in Sierra Leone had in the new day of independence. He spoke plainly of the many politicians who seek only money and power for themselves, and called upon the Native Administration officials and the people of the Kagboro Chiefdom to support their Chief, and to work hard and with honesty to improve their chieftaincy and their country, under the rule of God.

Rev. Fergusson conducted the meaningful service of installation and dedication, as he presented to the Chief her staff, and also a gift of a Bible.

After the service guests were served with a delicious meal of roast chicken, salad, Jollof rice with oysters, and cake. Visitors went to greet the Chief, and there was drumming and dancing and the occasional explosion of fireworks as the celebration continued.

Madam Bailor-Caulker did many good things for her chieftaincy. Among other things she encouraged salt mining, organized a fishing cooperative, and assisted in the formation of the Sierra Leone Federation of Women's Organizations, which provided opportunities for training for women. One of the most useful things she did was to arrange for a good road to be constructed between Moyamba and Shenge. This opened the way for transport of agricultural and fishing products, and for easy travel between Moyamba, the district headquarters town, and her headquarters.

Needless to say, I was one of the many who attended the installation and dedication service. It was a very interesting and exciting occasion.

Madam Honoria Bailor-Caulker processing to the church

The Sermon–Dr. S. M. Renner

Rev. B. A. Carew and Harford School Choir

Installation and Consecration–Rev. J. K. Fergusson

Installation and Consecration–Rev. J. K. Fergusson

Receiving the Staff

P.C. Honoina Bailor-Caulker with court messenger

The Chief with her Children (Back) Mervin, Hilton
(Front) Chad, Esther, Honoria, Chico

The Bailor Family with the new Paramount Chief

Chapter XIII. Saying Goodby

Not long after the momentous event described in the last chapter, several people retired and returned to the United States. Rev. Charles and Bertha Leader left after thirty-five years of service; then Dr. Silver, after thirty-four years.   Then on the 16th of June 1962, I embarked on the *M.V. Accra* for Liverpool. From there I toured in England and some of the Continent, and left Europe on the *Rotterdam* on August 8. It was painful in some ways to leave Sierra Leone, which had been my home since January of 1951, but I was looking forward to graduate study at Hartford Seminary Foundation in Hartford, Connecticut. I thought at the time that it might be my last time in Sierra Leone, but that was not to be. With church union with the Methodist Church in 1968, to form The United Methodist Church, I was asked to be on the staff of the World Division of the Board of Missions. My responsibilities as Area Executive Secretary for North and West Africa included Sierra Leone, so I made a trip there each year for four years, though in a different capacity than previously. Then from 1973-1980 I was a missionary in Ghana, and visited Sierra Leone two or three times during those years. After returning again to the U.S. I, along with Florence Barnhart, Elaine Gasser, and her friend Joyce Anderegg, returned in 1986 to celebrate our friend Madam Honoria Bailor-Caulker's 25th anniversary as chief. And in 1989 I spent three months in Sierra Leone as a volunteer as I began a year of volunteer work in five different countries in Africa after I retired from my work in Mississippi.

Those of us who were in Sierra Leone keep in touch. Many of our friends visit the United States at one time or another, or have come here to live, some as refugees, and so Sierra Leone is still in my heart and mind, more than fifty years after I first arrived in that land.

Epilogue

Much has changed in both the church and the country since the events related here occurred. During the twelve years I was there control of the church was gradually being turned over to national leadership. In February of 1973 Sierra Leone became an Affiliated Autonomous Conference at the first General Conference, held in Freetown. Rev. B. A. Carew was elected Bishop. When T. S. Bangura was later elected to succeed him, the Conference decided to become part of The United Methodist Church, and so is now a Central Conference of the U.M.C. The current Bishop (as of this writing in 2004) is a former student of mine at Trinity College in Ghana, Bishop J. C. Humper.

For many years the leadership of all the institutions and all the pastors have been Sierra Leoneans. There are very few missionaries. A great deal has been done by volunteers. Particularly remarkable is the founding by Dr. Lowell Gess and the continuation, in spite of great difficulties during the war, of the Kissi Eye Clinic in Freetown. He has seen that the clinic was provided with eye surgeons from volunteers. He then trained a Sierra Leone doctor who has continued the work, with help from volunteers. There is also a clinic and maternity center at Kissi. A hospital is now under construction, including a medical unit. Operation Classroom has provided much help with schools, medical work, and training in counseling to help deal with the huge problem of young people who have known nothing but war, and have seen their families killed or maimed or have killed themselves.

For the years since 1990 have been tragic ones for Sierra Leone. Only in 2003 was peace achieved in the vicious civil war. ECOWAS, the West African peacekeeping force, and one of the largest contingent of UN peacekeepers ever sent to one country, have been instrumental. There will soon be elections. Trials will soon begin for war criminals. A "Truth and Reconciliation Commission," chaired by Bishop Humper, similar to the one is South Africa, has begun to function. England has helped to train a new army and police force. However, the web-site *Sierra Leone News* reports that the International Crisis Group (ICG) in September (2003) stated that "the Sierra Leone government has made little progress in implementing institutional reforms and addressing problems such as poor governance, the capacity of the country's security forces, and corruption." The country faces tremendous problems. Thousands of persons were killed, thousands others maimed (one of the favorite means of punishment by the rebels was to chop off appendages, even of babies). Many more were, and some still are, refugees. A whole generation of young people has been without education and has known only fighting and fear. Much of the infrastructure has been destroyed–schools, hospitals, roads. I have grieved since hearing that not only Rotifunk Hospital, but the whole village of Rotifunk was destroyed. On our former hospital compound only the church remains. It was damaged, but has been repaired. I cannot bear to think of what has happened to all the people we knew, to my home for so many years.

****

Persons mentioned in this narrative who were living at the time but are now deceased are:
Walter and Edna Schutz, Dr. Mabel Silver, Mr. A. M. Bailor and P.C. Madam Honoria Bailor-Caulker, Cora Horst, Dr. S. M. Renner, Dr. Richard Caulker, Morlai Turay, Mrs. Priscilla Caulker, Lucy and Ellen Caulker, Les Shirley, Grace Shirley, Bishop B. A. Carew, Betty Carew, Rev. T. B. Williams, Chief A.T. Caulker and Chief William Caulker, Marjorie Hager, Ernest Kroma, Alfred Kroma, Betty Beveridge, Dr. Al French, Dr. Donald Megill, Rev. and Mrs. Leader, Bishop I. D. Warner, Mrs. S. S. Hough, Nora Vesper, Rev. W. B. Claye, Waveline Babbitt, June Hartranft, Mary McLanachan, Sir Milton Margai, Rev. J. K. Fergusson, Dr. Carl Heinmiller, Marion Caulker. There may be others who have died. This is most certainly true of our Sierra Leone friends, for so many were killed and we have heard from only a few.

I thank God for their lives of loving service.

Of the many I knew in Sierra Leone, there are two who were especially important to me. I want to share more of their stories here.

Mabel Silver: A Doctor Who Served Sierra Leone With Compassion and Courage

"It's wonderful the way God sees us through many circumstances."

Dr. Mabel Silver often testified to her sense of God's presence, as she recounted some of the story of her 30 years served in Sierra Leone, West Africa, as a missionary of the United Brethren in Christ, later Evangelical United Brethren, and now the United Methodist Church.

When asked in 1969 to tell some of her story and record it, she began, "I was born in Baltimore, Maryland, March 23, 1902. I had the usual elementary and high school education. I had planned to go to normal school, as it was called in those days, to train as a teacher. If I had been permitted to carry out that plan, I would probably still be teaching in elementary school. However, I was not permitted to carry on with this program that I'd planned, because an uncle advised my father that for people in our circumstances, I had had enough education for a girl, and I had better get out and get a job and help support the family. So I went to work for several years as a file clerk with the American Railway Express Company.

106

"I belonged to a local church (Fulton Avenue United Methodist Church, Baltimore) which has always had an intense interest in mission, and from the time I was a child I was involved in missionary organizations, first for children and the Otterbein Guild and then the Women's Missionary Association. Through the reading course and through mission study classes I learned a great deal about medical missions. Through one book particularly, *A Crusade of Compassion for the Healing of the Nations*, I became very interested in medical missions. It seemed unreasonable to me, but I had a growing sense of feeling that God was calling me to study medicine and go abroad to Africa as a medical missionary. At the time I could have thought of nothing more unreasonable. I had no money for education, I was not a particularly courageous person, by no means a pioneer; and yet I could not get away from the feeling that this was the plan God had for my life. Finally, I said, "Well, I can't see how this can happen, but if it is Your will for me, I am willing to along with it!"

"For the last few months of my work as a clerk, I saved as much money as I could. I talked to the pastor of the church about this, and arrangements were made for me to enter Lebanon Valley College. I worked at various jobs during the summers and during the school year and graduated from Lebanon Valley in 1925 with a Bachelor of Science degree. I entered the University of Maryland School of Medicine in 1925, where I was the only woman in my class of medicine. The class at that point numbered 131. Four years later, we finished [with] 101 [students]; I was the *one* in each case.

"It was an interesting experience, a very trying one in spots. Certainly, if I had not felt that God was calling me to work in Sierra Leone, I would never have lasted out the first few months of medical school. By the grace of God, and by the amazing cooperation of the church to which I belonged, my education was finished. After two years of hospital work in Baltimore, I went to the University of London where I took my diploma in Tropical Medicine and Hygiene. In the spring of 1932, I went out to Sierra Leone to work in the clinic there–actually, to relieve a nurse (Miss Nora Vesper) who had operated the clinic and who was going on leave.

"This was a completely new experience, of course. This was not a hospital. There were no trained staff; I was the whole staff. We did have one girl, I think, who was on salary at the time, who acted as an interpreter. There were many languages. English was the language of education and government, but in dealing with people who came to the clinic we were dealing with people of some 17 or 18 different tribes. We had an interesting time sometimes in finding somebody to interpret for us–but it was amazing how God undergirded us in those days. We had one ward with three beds; there was no office or examining room. There were two rooms in this dispensary, which had been used, one as a bedroom and one as a living room, for the nurse through the years she had worked there. We finally converted one of these into an office and the other one into a maternity ward. This dispensary had been built in 1904, I believe, as a memorial to Drs. Hatfield and Archer (two women) who had been killed in the uprising of '98."

Dr. Silver, after she returned from her first leave, worked for two years in Taiama, but then it was decided that she should return to Rotifunk, and it was there the hospital was eventually built and where she spent the rest of her life in Sierra Leone.

One important aspect of the medical work was the baby clinic, which had been started by Nora Vesper. When Dr. Silver arrived in 1932, they thought they did very well if they had a dozen or fifteen mothers and babies; by the time she left Sierra Leone in 1962, the baby clinic had grown to two clinics a week, caring for 500-700 babies.

In 1956 a very simple, cement hospital was dedicated, which included a laboratory, a pharmacy, a delivery room, male and female wards, a maternity unit, and a surgical room. "Even though I was not a surgeon," said Dr. Silver, "and we did not have a surgeon in sight, we had faith there would be one."

In 1953 a nurse-midwife came from England, sent by the Evangelical United Brethren Board in the United States, and a school of midwifery was started to train African women as midwives.

Dr. Silver soon became famous for, as she said, "producing babies where babies had not been produced before. The African woman has lived in vain if she hasn't produced a child. . . . It was interesting that the very first patient who came to, as far as I can recall, with this problem, was a Lebanese woman who had been married for some six years (however, she was married when she was only 14), and had not become pregnant. I did not usually examine the male, but she was so desperate that I agreed to see whether her husband was capable of reproducing and discovered that he was. And so I thought that they didn't need any medication at all. Actually, she did have a problem with constipation, so we gave her some Extract of Cascara. She went home and in less than a year produced a son. You would know that the medicine had nothing on earth to do with that; it was probably just the faith–there is a psychological factor, I am sure, in this business, just as there is in many other experiences in life, and the people came because they felt that we had the answer. It was largely because of their faith rather than anything remarkable we did."

But she was not only a doctor for women and children; she treated all manner of diseases. In 1952, patients attending the clinic numbered 55,000; in 1960, 66,000. This did not include prenatal or baby clinic, or attendance at the leprosy clinics which were also started under her management. During many of these years she was the only doctor, sometimes the only trained medical staff. In later years there were a nurse-midwife and a medical technologist. Male doctors (including finally a surgeon) did not arrive in Rotifunk until a few years before she retired.

As she reminisced about the years in the land she loved, she continued, "African sleeping sickness is one of the most dramatic things to treat that one would ever see. It's quite different from what is referred to in temperate climates as sleeping sickness . . . I did not know in my early years in Sierra Leone that sleeping sickness, or trypanasomiasis, existed there. I went to Conference one year, and one of the pastors said to me, "When are you going back to Rotifunk?"

"I told him, and asked why; he answered, 'Well, I left my son there sick.'"

She returned to Rotifunk, but didn't plan to open the clinic the day she got back. She continued, "We didn't get back until early afternoon; I thought I'd get my house in order and start properly the next morning. But this man came from Shenge, 60 miles down the river, and he wanted to go down with the tide. He sent a note and asked if I would see his son, so that he would know what the situation was, and I said, yes, I would. So I went over to the clinic to see this young man, who was about 20 or 21. As he came along he looked very dull; he was dragging one foot and one hand was rather limp. He sat down and immediately fell asleep.

"I said to his father, 'Well, this looks to me like sleeping sickness; but it's too dark now to see anything under the microscope (we didn't have electricity in those days.) If you will come over tomorrow morning I will check his blood, and see."

"I didn't know how lucky I was; it's very difficult to find the trypanasome in the blood. But the next morning in the first fresh drop I put under the microscope, there were these creatures, flipping and flopping, and the diagnosis was made. But not knowing that we had trypanasomiasis in Sierra Leone, I didn't have the drug in hand to treat it. So I sent to the government medical department in Freetown. Believe it or not, it took ten days to get that medicine 55 miles from Freetown. . . . In the meantime, the man became completely unconscious . . .

"(When the medicine finally came) I went over to the clinic, sterilized the syringe . . . and gave it to him intramuscularly. It took two people to hold him to keep him from rolling back on the syringe, he was so far out, or comatose. You can imagine my amazement, then, almost as great as that of the Africans, when the next morning I went out to see what had happened, and he had got up and walked out in the back yard, and was sitting talking with his friends and eating."

Dr. Silver laughed, and told another story of a similar experience. A man, stiff from top to toe, was brought on the river to Rotifunk, and then carried up to the clinic on a door. The doctor checked his blood, but was not lucky this time to find the trypanasomes. Finally, however, because she didn't know what else it could be, she gave him an injection for sleeping sickness. The next morning when she went to see the patient, the section chief who had sent him was there with some of his friends. This time, too, the patient was sitting up, talking and eating rice. The chief, who had apparently tried for several days to persuade the man to come to the hospital, and finally sent him when he was unconscious said, "Didn't I tell you Silver has the biggest devil in the country?" Chuckling, Dr. Silver added, "A rather strange commentary on a Christian missionary!"

To recount even a small part of her experiences would take many more pages; the story of the morning in 1942 when word spread throughout the country that she had died (when she had been seriously ill with typhoid); and of the heart attack in 1953 when the medical technologist was the only other missionary with her at Rotifunk. Even during those hours of pain, while arrangements were being made to take her to the hospital in Freetown on a freight train, she wrote orders for patients in the hospital, and was more concerned about causing trouble for the staff than what might happen to her.

In 1953 Queen Elizabeth bestowed on Dr. Silver The Order of the British Empire. In March of 1971 she was honored by the Honorable John Akar, Ambassador from Sierra Leone to the United States (formerly from Rotifunk), at a birthday dinner in Washington, D.C. It was also the occasion of Sierra Leone's tenth anniversary of independence.

But most meaningful to her were the celebrations and gifts given her by the paramedical staff, and the mothers who attended the clinics with their babies. The mothers gave as a parting gift the equivalent of nearly $100–a large amount compared to their resources. In this way they honored her as traditionally a chief was honored, with money for the journey.

She left Sierra Leone in 1962; after two years of itinerating and speaking in churches, she worked for more than five years in the Rosewood State Hospital in Maryland, a hospital for the mentally retarded.

When Dr. Silver left us, she went as she would have wanted. She had often spoken of not wanting to live so long that she would be a burden to others. On Maundy Thursday evening of 1972, she attended a Communion service in her church. On Good Friday morning her friend of many years who lived in the same apartment building found her, realized that she had had a stroke, and took her to the hospital. Easter Sunday, April 2, 1972, was truly Resurrection Day for her.

There were two memorial services held for her in Sierra Leone, one in Freetown and one in Rotifunk where she lived for so many years. The church in Rotifunk was packed by her many friends, some of whom were brought into the world by her help, and most, if not all the rest, helped at some time during her life there. Many were helped not only in a physical way, but by her Christian concern. While Christians remembered her especially in a Sunday service, the Muslims of the town had their special remembrance the following Friday. Truly her Christian influence was felt by all.

Her own words make a fitting conclusion to her story:

"God had been wonderfully good in undergirding and enabling me to see through many difficult situations. I am profoundly grateful to have had the opportunity to have spent my working years in a place where the practice of medicine was so fascinating and where it was so wonderfully appreciated, many times out of all proportion to what one was able to do."

–Based on a recording of an interview with Dr. Silver by Esther Megill, and written by her for an article in the October 1983 *Response* magazine. Used by permission of *Response.*

Honoria Bailor-Caulker:

"Give her credit for all she did . . ."

May 8, 1962 was a great day in Shenge, in Sierra Leone, West Africa. Then Honoria Bailor, known by many Evangelical United Brethren women in the United States, and a leader of women in Sierra Leone, was installed as Madam Honoria Bailor-Caulker, Paramount Chief of the Kargboro Chiefdom. Hundreds of people traveled the roads to Shenge on that day to attend the formal installation and dedication service. Many E.U.B. missionaries, paramount chiefs, ambassadors, and other government officials, as well as members of the Caulker family and many of her subjects, were present to give honor to the new chief.

Since the roof of the Shenge church had been removed in preparation for renovation, a roof of palm branches, bamboo, and sticks decorated with brilliantly colored tropical leaves made a pleasant shade within the church building. Only a small part of the crowd could sit in the church, while others sat on benches outside under palm shelters.

The service began with a procession of the Chief, followed by her tribal authorities and family members, with a guard of honor of the local Boy Scouts and Girl Guides and court messengers. The Sierra Leone Police Band furnished the music. The Rev. J.K. Fergusson of Moyamba conducted the service. The Rev B. A. Crew, superintendent of the Bo District (later the first bishop of the autonomous church), and other pastors and missionaries took part. Dr. S. M. Renner, Superintendent of the Freetown District, challenged the Chief to rule her people in justice, tempered with mercy. Rev. Fergusson conducted the meaningful service of installation and dedication, as he presented to the Chief her staff, and a gift of a Bible. After the service there was feasting, drumming, dancing, and fireworks in celebration.

Madame Bailor-Caulker had been elected on December 18, 1961. The Sherbro people elect women as well as men as chiefs, if they are descendants of a chief, through either the maternal or paternal sides. Honoria's grandmother, Lucy B. Caulker (daughter of Chief Thomas Stephen Caulker), at age fourteen was one of the first two persons to become Christian at the United Brethren mission in Shenge. Her grave is behind the Gomer Memorial United Methodist Church.

The church is a historic one, a memorial to Joseph Gomer, an African-American from Dayton, Ohio, who was sent with his wife, Mary, to Sierra Leone in 1871. The United Brethren Board had almost given up on the mission field in Africa (begun in 1855), because so many missionaries had died. However, after much prayer they sent the Gomers. Through their efforts the mission was well established, but Joseph Gomer died there. Lucy Caulker's grave is next to his.

The film *Amistad* tells the story of the beginning of Christianity among the Mende people in Sierra Leone. What the movie does not tell is how the American Missionary Society (Congregational Church), who sent missionaries with the returning Sierra Leoneans, within a few years arranged with the United Brethren to take over their work along with the work at Shenge.

Long before she became a chief, Honoria Remmie was a teacher in Evangelical United Brethren schools in Sierra Leone. She was one of the first two women to attend the teacher's college at what was then Fourah Bay College (now the University of Sierra Leone). She then married A. Max Bailor, who was a school teacher, then headmaster, and finally the first Sierra Leonean to become Conference Education Secretary in the E.U.B. Church. Honoria with marriage also became a mother of his five children. She and her husband then had seven children, five of whom lived to adulthood.

With the organization of a conference Women's Society of World Service in Sierra Leone, Mrs. Bailor became the first president. She was a guest and speaker at the E.U.B. W.S.W.S. Quadrennial Convention in Harrisonburg, Virginia, September 17-21, 1958, and visited several other churches in the following weeks. She expressed thanks for the missionaries who had come to her country, who made it possible for her grandmother and many others after her, including herself, to become Christian. Mrs. Bailor spoke of the growing W.S.W.S., and of their special project: to educate girls at Harford School.[1] She herself graduated from Harford School for Girls, which has educated many leaders in the church and the nation.

Honoria was interested in becoming part of the political process in her country. In 1958, just before coming to the United States, she canvassed for election to parliament, hoping to be the first woman Member of Parliament. She lost that election, but later did become an M.P. (Member of Parliament) in the '70's and served until a one-party government was formed by the opposition party.

Madame Honoria did a great deal for her people in the Chiefdom, and for the women of Sierra Leone. She attended conferences, seminars and meetings in and out of Sierra Leone. In 1995 she represented the Sierra Leone government at the Fourth World Conference on Women in Beijing, China.

In her Chiefdom she encouraged communal labor, organized a fishing cooperative, used her influence to start a secondary school, and was able to get the International Labor Organization to pave the road from Moyamba to Shenge. This made a great difference because improved transportation allowed for the transport of food and other goods.

As Chief, she visited each Section of the Chiefdom at intervals. Dancers, singers and drummers would meet her, and she would be carried in a hammock to the Court *barrie*. Her orderly and hornblower (who announced the arrival of the Chief), the Speaker, Chiefdom councillors, and other dignitaries would accompany her. The section chief and people of the Section she was visiting would greet them, take her to her lodging, and dance all night enjoying themselves. In the morning all the men, women, and children would meet at the Court *barrie*. She addressed the crowd on many issues affecting the Chiefdom, and received any questions they had. The officials of that Section would then take her to the next, where she would again be welcomed and celebrated as before.

---

[1] The report of her message is found in *The World Evangel*, January 1959, pp. 13ff.

On December 21, 1986, the writer and other former missionaries and special friends of Honoria (Florence Barnhart and Elaine Gasser, and a friend, Joyce Anderegg, who was a consultant for the Women's Division) had the privilege of helping her celebrate the twenty-fifth anniversary of her crowning as Chief. The Silver Jubilee Thanksgiving Service, held in the Gomer Memorial Church in Shenge, lasted for two hours. This was followed by good food, dancing, drumming, and the firing of a canon.[2]

Then, in 1991 civil war broke out in Sierra Leone, and continued until 2003. The effects on the lives of the people of that nation were catastrophic. In November of 1995 Madam Honoria was forced, for her own safety, to move to Freetown, along with chiefs from other chieftaincies. In 1997 there were a cease fire and an election, and it seemed that peace had come again. Madame Honoria wrote that "I was to go home in pomp and pageantry on the 27th of March 1997 for Easter, after being displaced for more than two years. I was involved in an accident due to the digging of the streets in Freetown. I was admitted at the Military Forces Hospital on the 24th of March 1997 . . . "

The fall had resulted in a broken hip. Soon after, war broke out again, and Freetown was isolated, with the blockading of the port, closing of the airport, and roads leading to the interior blocked by rebel forces. There were decreasing food and medical supplies. Having the surgery that could have taken care of the broken hip was not possible for her. For six months she lay in the hospital, while conditions worsened in Freetown and the entire country. Finally one of her sons, Chadwick, was able to get her to Guinea, where she remained as a refugee, along with some members of her family. Refugees have little or no source of income, and can exist only with the help of friends from outside or whatever help the U.N. or other organizations can give them. A number of Madam Honoria's friends supplied her with money to pay for rent and other support.

However, her physical condition continued to deteriorate. She and her son were sure that she could be helped if she came to the U.S. for medical treatment. He managed, with the aid of some of his friends, to get them here the fall of 1998. With the help of the pastor of the Biltmore United Methodist Church, and some United Methodist medical persons in Asheville, North Carolina, plans were made for surgery. However, it was obvious when she arrived that she was in no condition for surgery. Eventually, her son took her back to Silver Spring, Maryland. There she died on the evening of Sierra Leone's 38th Independence Anniversary, April 27, 1999. A memorial service was held for her on May 8, with Bishop J. C. Humper, Bishop of The United Methodist Church in Sierra Leone, as the preacher. Her body was taken to Sierra Leone for eventual burial beside her grandmother behind Gomer Memorial Church in Shenge. With her passage has gone a beloved leader of her country, her Chieftaincy, and her Church. Her influence will live on, although those who love her grieve at her passing.

Give her credit for all she [did]. She deserves the respect of everyone.
Proverbs 31:31, <u>Good News Bible</u>

--Esther Megill

---

[2]An article describing this event written by Elaine Gasser may be found in *Response,* June 1987, pp. 8ff.

Dictionary

Barrie–An open building, with a roof and walls a few feet high, used for gatherings in a village or a compound.

Buba–An article of clothing like a blouse, used with a lappa in traditional Sierra Leone dress.

Bundu or Sande Society –The secret society for women. At 13 or 14 a girl's parents received a small piece of tobacco, indicating that the Sande session(the term used by Mendes, called Bundu by the Temne and other tribes) is about to begin. She and other girls her age are whitened all over with clay, and dressed in locally dyed blue Gara (indigo) cloth, and are taken by the older women to the bush. Traditionally, they spent many months there, where they were taught weaving, basket-making, and domestic science. They were taught ceremonial dances suitable for all occasions, and also taught obedience, cheerfulness, and respect for elders, including for the middle-aged and elderly husbands who were awaiting their graduation. The Bundu devil was present for many of the dances. During their time there, clitorectomy or female circumcision was performed. In more modern times the length of time is shortened because many of the girls are in school. However, the sense of belonging and comradeship is very strong. Even many Christian girls go through Bundu, although the Caulker family never did. During the time I was in Sierra Leone, at least, the Bundu or Sande Society was very influential.[17] (This society is also present in Liberia.)

Calabash–a type of gourd or pod that grows wild in most parts of Africa. Many useful items are made from them. For example, rice is washed in a calabash, fruit or other items carried in them, or they are used in other ways around the house.

Creole print–a distinctive dress originated by the Creole women in Freetown, but worn in other parts of Sierra Leone also. It was made from cotton cloth printed with designs, frequently African in origin, and had appliqued designs at the top, sometimes made from lace, or just patterns made by sewing. Usually one wore "carpet slippers" with these. They were slippers made by needlepoint, often with patterns to match the print with which they were to be worn. They had leather soles.

Jigger–A jigger is the result of the penetration of a flea (often carried by birds) into one's toes or feet. The flea then lays eggs, and an egg sack develops, which itches. It must be removed carefully, for if the sac bursts infection easily follows.

Lappa–A straight piece of cloth, which could have many different designs, approximately 40" wide and two yards long. The woman wraps this around her from the waist down. Such cloths are also used to tie her baby on her back.

Poro Society–A secret society for men, among the Mende, Sherbro, Vai, and some of the Konos and Temnes. (And also in Liberia.) At a certain time each year the Poro drums were heard in the bush, and senior members of the society came into the town to take the boys away to be initiated. They were circumcised, and in the past would stay in the bush for months or years. Here they learned many things useful for the society–formerly, they were trained to be warriors. They also learned skills such as farming, basket making, weaving, fishing, pottery, etc. They learned traditions of their tribe, drumming, singing and acrobatics. There was sex education. Above all, the boy (who was now becoming a man) learned comradeship with his fellow initiates. Although with the expansion of education and schools the time was shortened to only a few weeks or days, it was still quite powerful, even politically, at the time I was in Sierra Leone.[18]

Wari–A game played with a board of the type shown in the photo. There are two parallel rows of holes of six each. The game is played with seeds, pebbles, marbles or ivory balls used as game pieces. Sometimes boys even scoop holes in the earth and play with them. There are two players, each sitting on one side of the board, facing his set of six holes. Into each of the holes are placed four game pieces. The game proceeds by a player picking up the four seeds from any of his six holes, and in counter clockwise direction, drops one seed in each of the holes which follow the one from which he picked up his seeds. He then picks up all the seeds from the hole into which he dropped the last of the four seeds. He continues to play until he comes to an empty hole. He drops into it the last seed in his hand. It is now the other player's turn, and the game proceeds with their playing alternately. The winner of the game is the player who succeeds in gaining all the sets of four seeds, or as many as possible, depending on the length of play agreed upon.

This game is played in many countries in Africa, and even in some other countries, such as India and the Philippines. They have a different name in each country. In Ghana the game is called "Oware" and in Liberia, "Poo."[19]

Endnotes

1. Information was obtained from *Independence!, Daily Mail Guide*, 1961, pp. 3-6; Christopher Fyfe, *A Short History of Sierra Leone*, London: Longman's, Green & Co. Ltd, c.1962, Chaps. 5 & 6; *Sierra Leone*, produced by the Director of Information, Sierra Leone Government, n.d., pp. 1-6, and personal experience.

2. Though I seldom wore it afterward!

3. See *A Short History of Sierra Leone* by Christopher Fyfe, p.144. London: Longman's, c1962.

4. The source of this article is unknown. It was no doubt in one of the E.U.B. Church publications.

5. Later, after Elaine Gasser arrived, I had to share this fame with her!

6. Credit must be given to Lois Olsen for her account of the Liberia trip in her book, *Contentment Is Great Gain: A Missionary Midwife in Sierra Leone,* published in 1996. I could find no letters I had written after November of 1961, and so her description (much more detailed than I have given here) helped me remember our experiences.

7. Esther Bailor Momoh has given her written permission for me to use this story.

8. Lowell A. Gess, *Mine Eyes Have Seen the Glory,* RLE Press, c.2002, p.59.

9. "Of Such is the Kingdom of God," an article in *The World Evangel*, date unknown (sometime in early 1960.)

10..Gess, op.cit., pp. 60-61.

11. See Lois Olsen, *Contentment Is Great Gain*, p. 99.

12. I was privileged to stay in the home of Mrs. Hough during the time I worked in Dayton, Ohio, as Director of the Central Girls Club. She was the president of the national Women's

Missionary Association for many years. Just before I left for Africa Mrs. Hough invited me and two friends who also rented rooms in her home for breakfast. I shall never forget that she read Psalm 121:8, "The Lord will keep your going out and your coming in from this time forth and for evermore."

13. Solomon Caulker died tragically in a plane crash off the coat of Dakar on August 26, 1960.

14. From "A Visit of the Deputation to Rotifunk," by Christiana Caulker, *The World Evangel*, April 1955, pp. 108-109.

15. The editorial was called "I Will Remember," but I have no date. It would have been written in early 1961.

16. *Independence! Daily Mail Guide*, written containing a program for the Independence Celebrations, p. 63.

17. See Roy Lewis, *Sierra Leone: A Modern Portrait*, London: His Majestey's Stationery Office, 1954, pp. 145ff.

18. Op. cit, pp. 129ff.

19. Christian, Angela, "Oware (Nam-Nam), a Ghanaian National Game," Accra: Advance Press Limited, n.d., pp. 7-11.